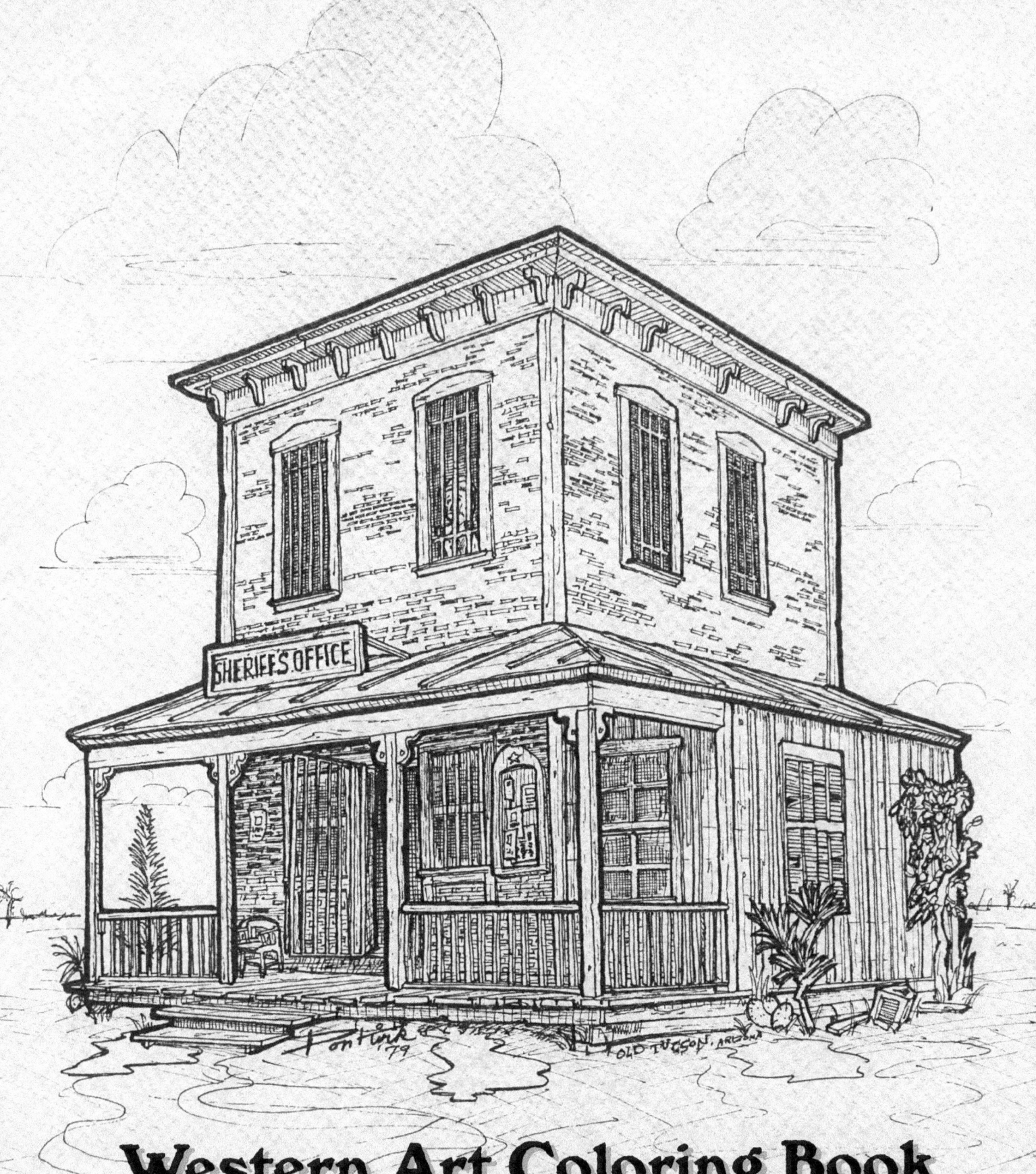

Western Art Coloring Book
Pen & Ink Old West Art (Vol II)
By Don Kirk

Western Art Coloring Book
Pen & Ink Old West Art (Vol II)
By Don Kirk

Published by
SWEETWATER STAGELINES™
An imprint of
THE OLD WEST COMPANY™
5118 Village Trail Drive
San Antonio, Texas 78218

Tradepaper (ISBN13): 978-0-9898004-5-7
Printed and bound in the United States of America

Other Pen & Ink Coloring Books By Don Kirk:
Western Art Coloring Book Volume I
Iron Horse Art Coloring Book
Sundry Art Coloring Book
Old West Photos at theoldwestcompany.com

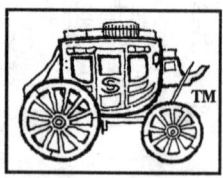

SWEETWATER STAGELINES™
SAN ANTONIO, TEXAS

Western Art Coloring Book
Pen & Ink Old West Art (Vol II)
By Don Kirk

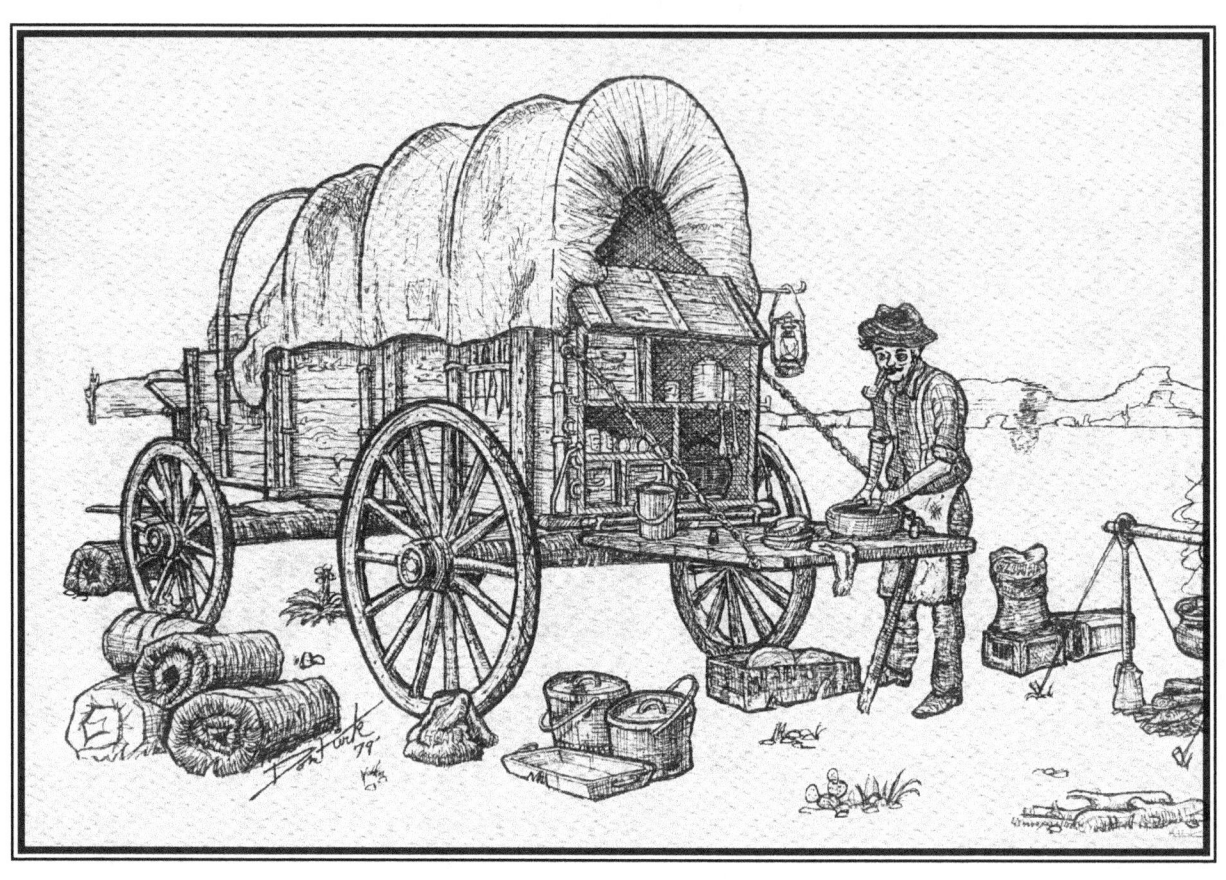

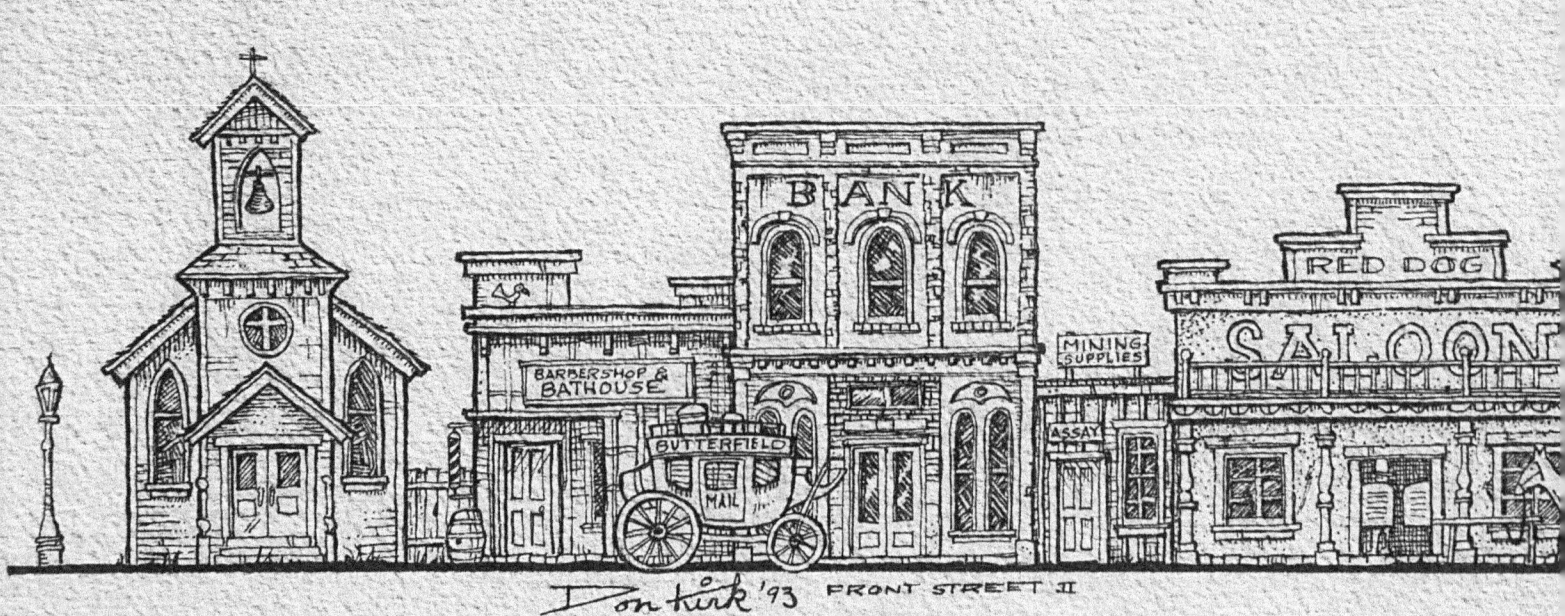

Don Kirk '93   FRONT STREET II

Don Kirk has been traveling the West for many years searching for the physical remains of the American West of the 1800's. He was looking for remnants that could unearth what life was like in a barren land and reveal how hard it was to survive and succeed. Just try to read a book and sew a blanket under a kerosine lantern. Don found many abandoned buildings with weathered clapboards sitting precariously on rotting cedar posts. He found desert towns with dilapidated boardwalks, squeaking windmills on the open plains, and boarded-up mine shafts. He found recreations of Old West villages built as movie sets for westerns and he drew from scratch fictional towns to be built for the next great western theme park. Don Kirk has been fascinated with the early American West ever since his father brought home a tiny black & white television set and sat there after dinner watching the TV westerns of the 1960s: shows like Gunsmoke, Maverick, Bonanza, The Rifleman, and Rawhide. These Pen & Inks were originally drawn back in the early 1990's for use on notecards, stationary, postcards, and art prints and this is the first reproduction of some of those works of art that you can use for coloring with pencil or crayon or for just looking at. Now you can flip through these pages and rediscover the Old West with Don Kirk's Western Art. Enjoy.

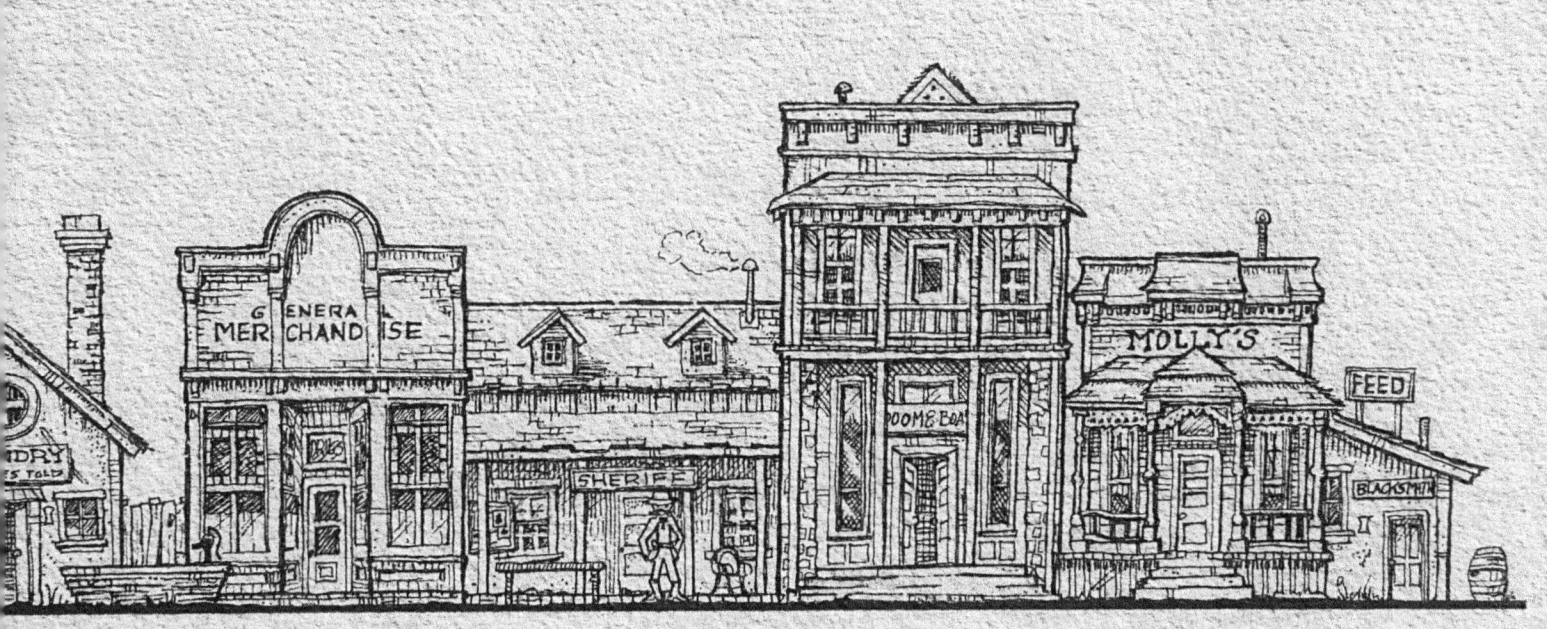

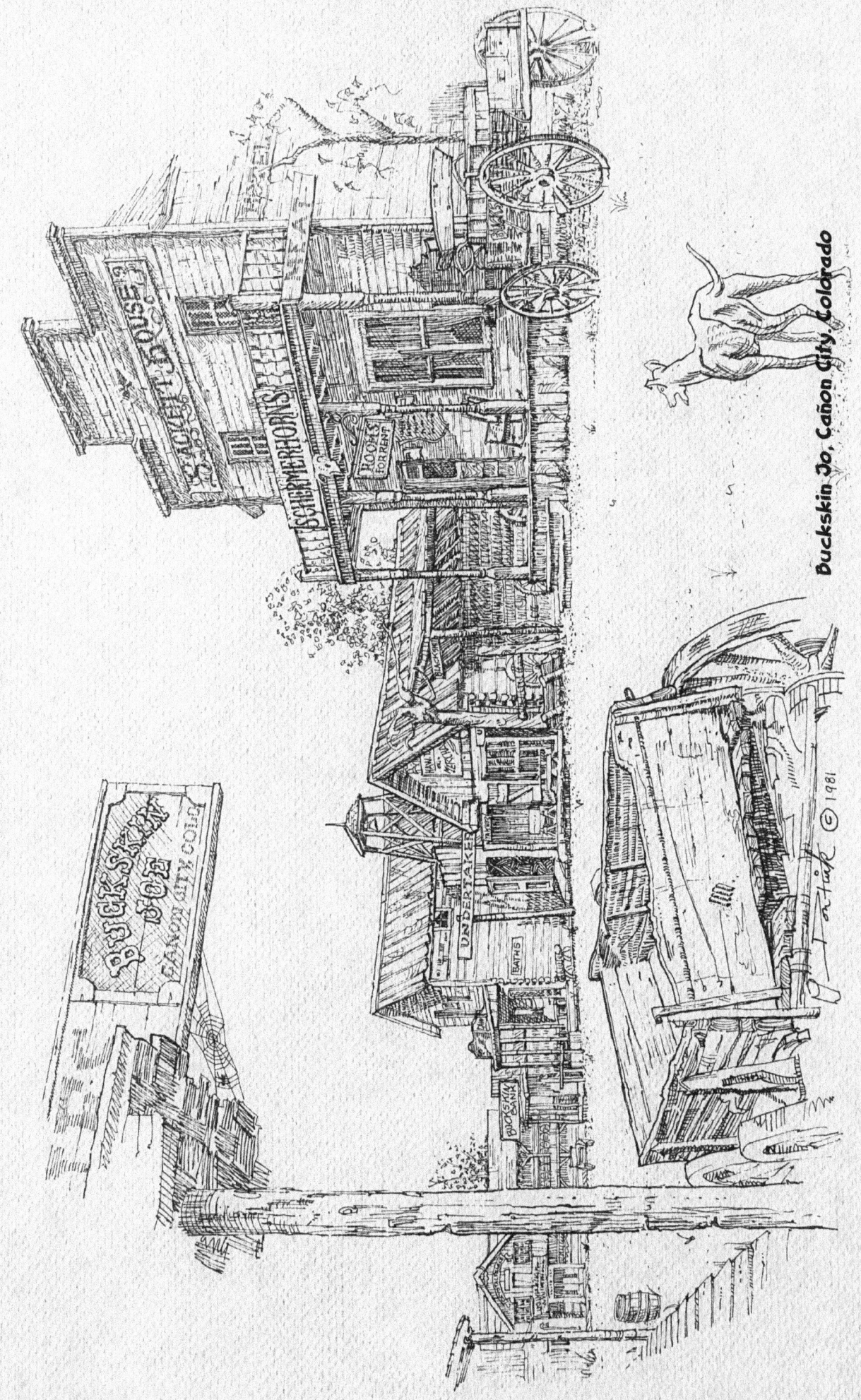

Buckskin Jo, Cañon City, Colorado

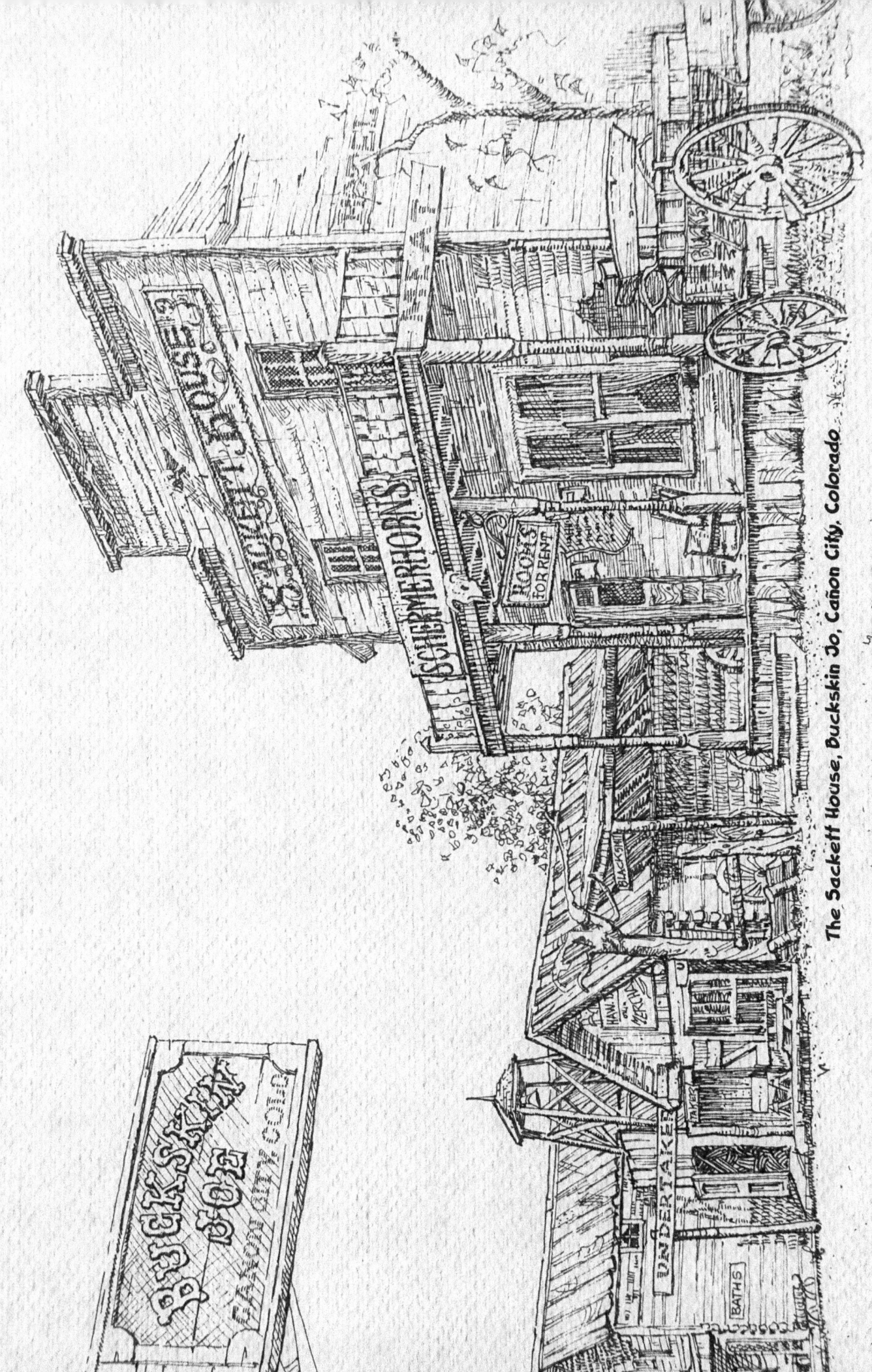

The Sackett House, Buckskin Jo, Cañon City, Colorado

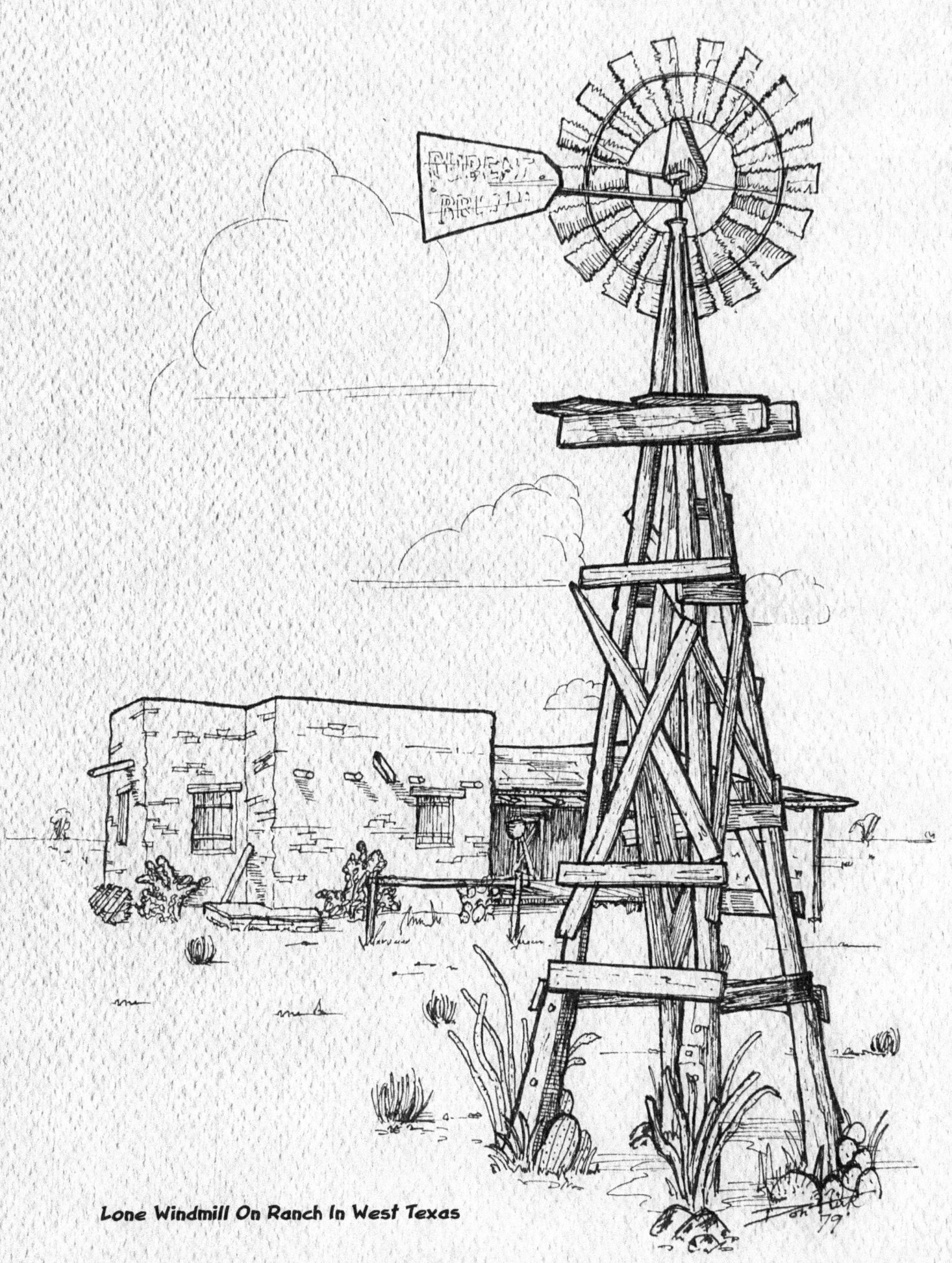

Lone Windmill On Ranch In West Texas

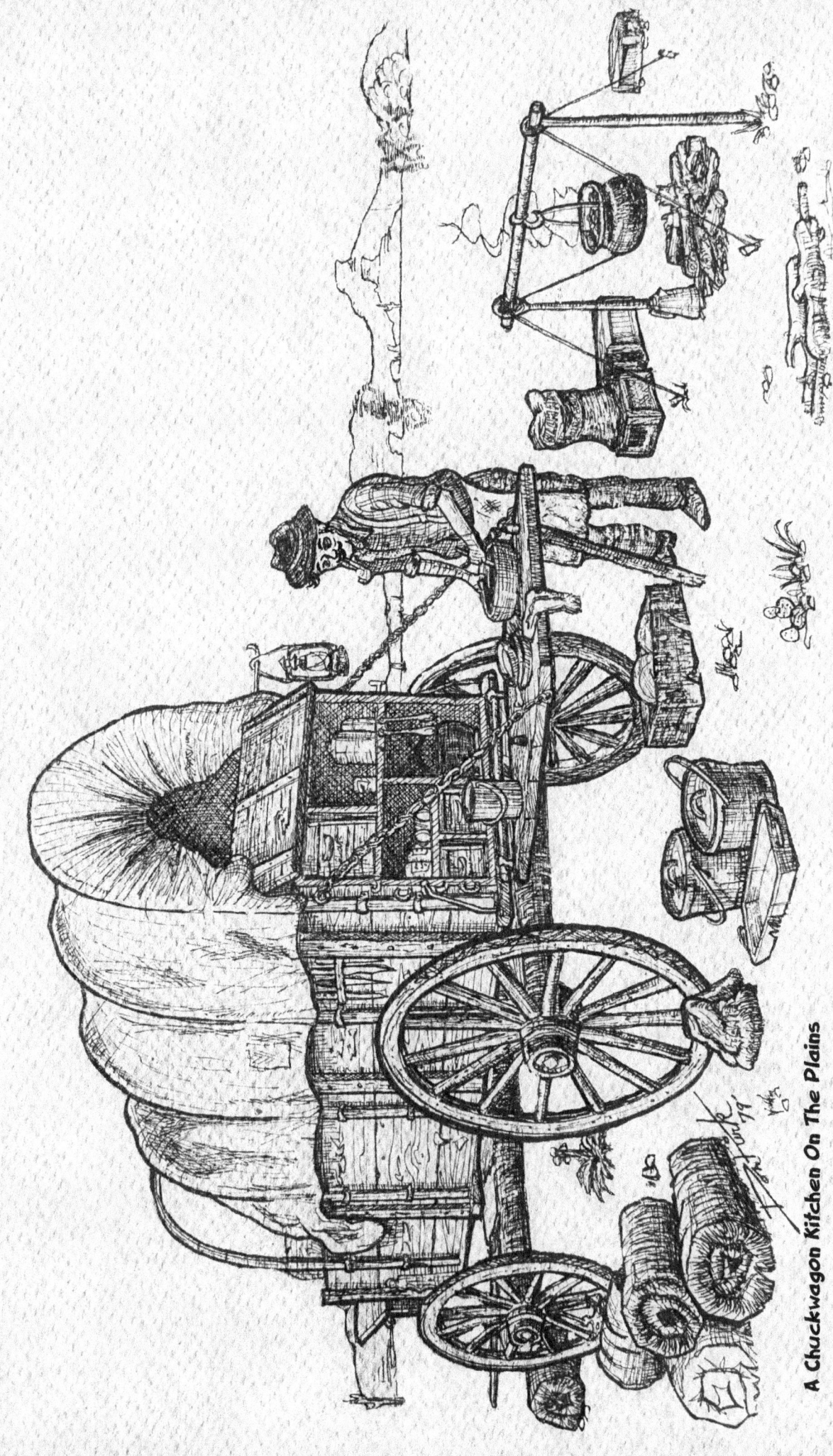

A Chuckwagon Kitchen On The Plains

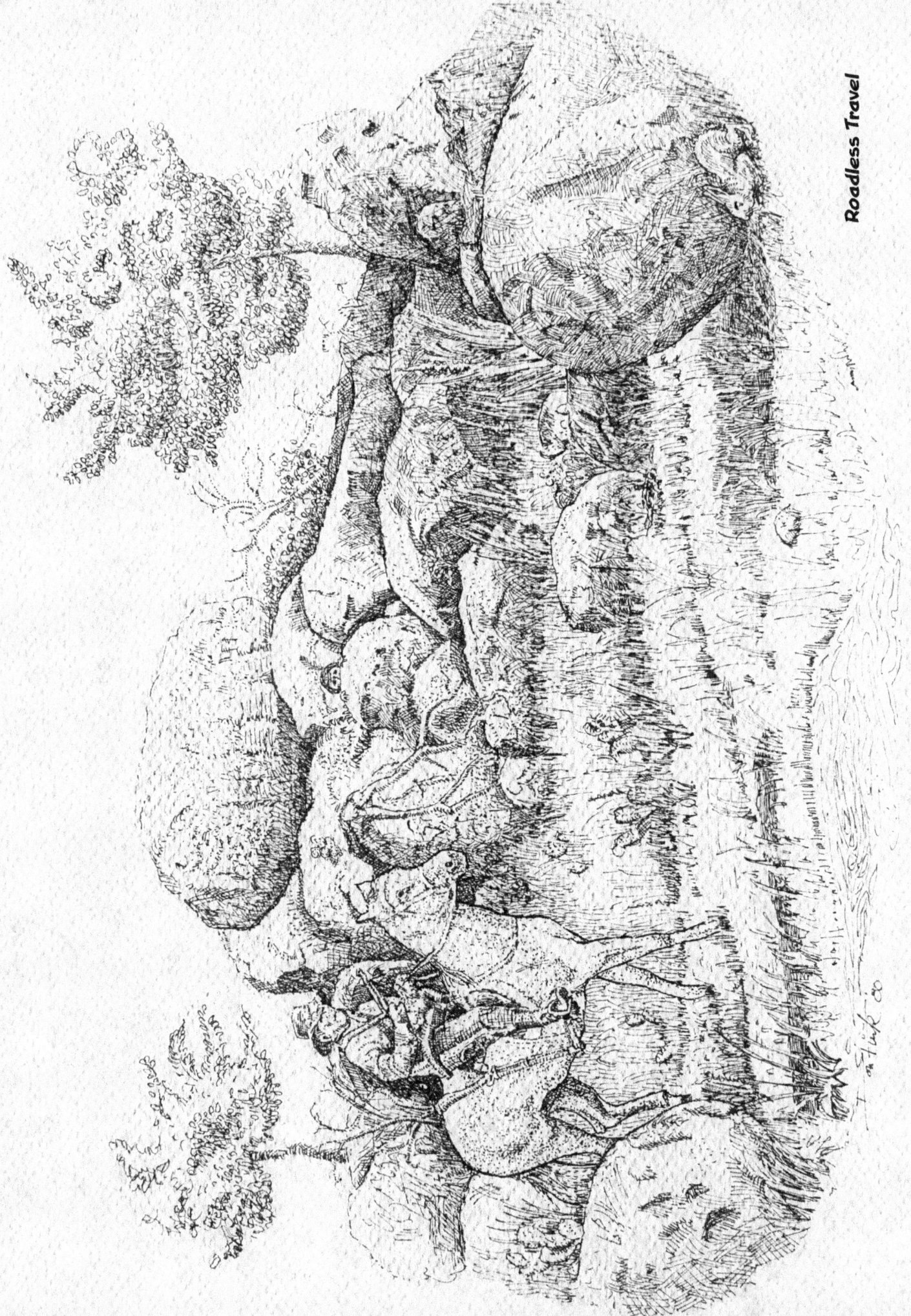

Roadless Travel

The Town Of Diablo, RedRock Canyon Territory

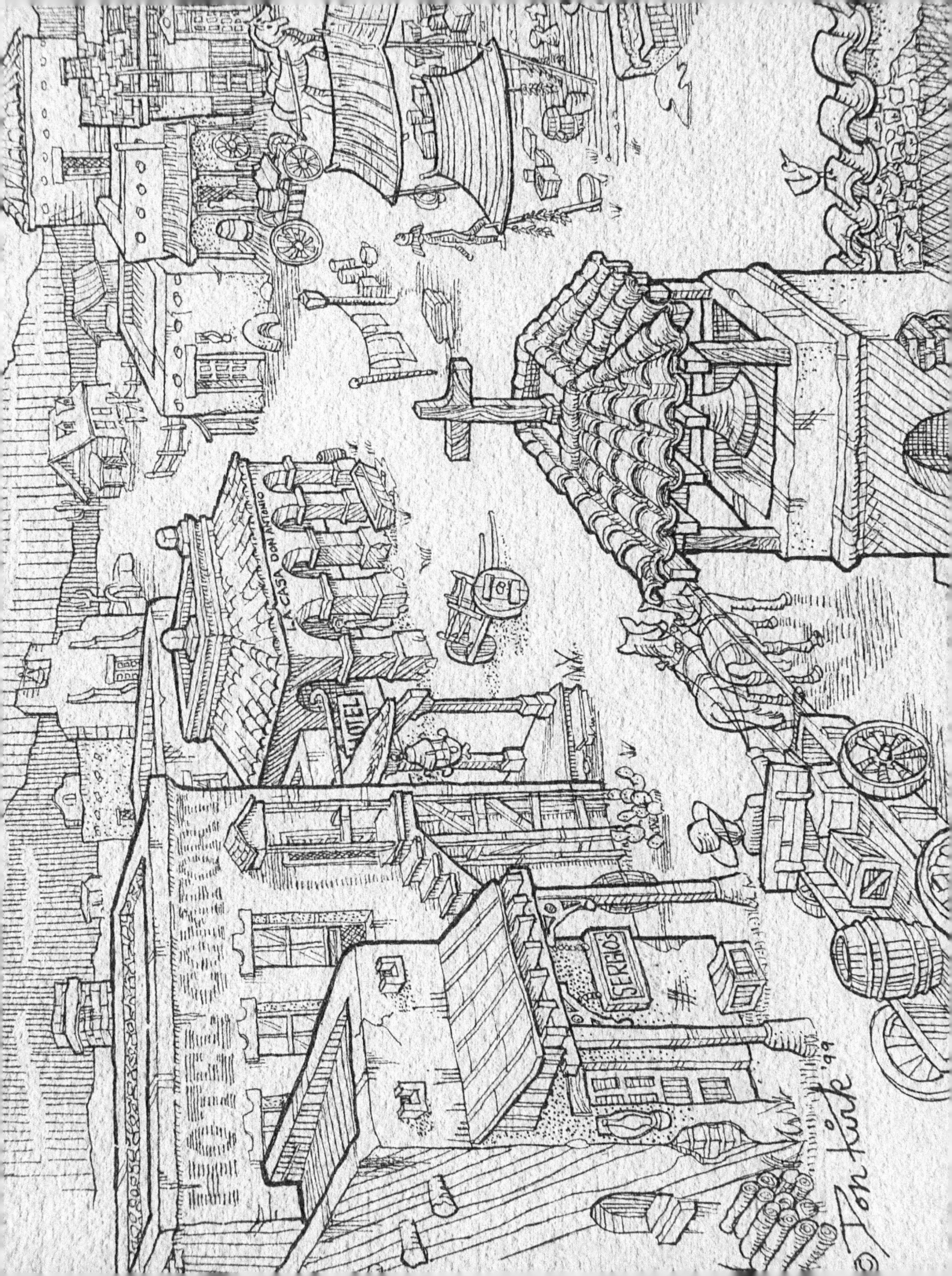

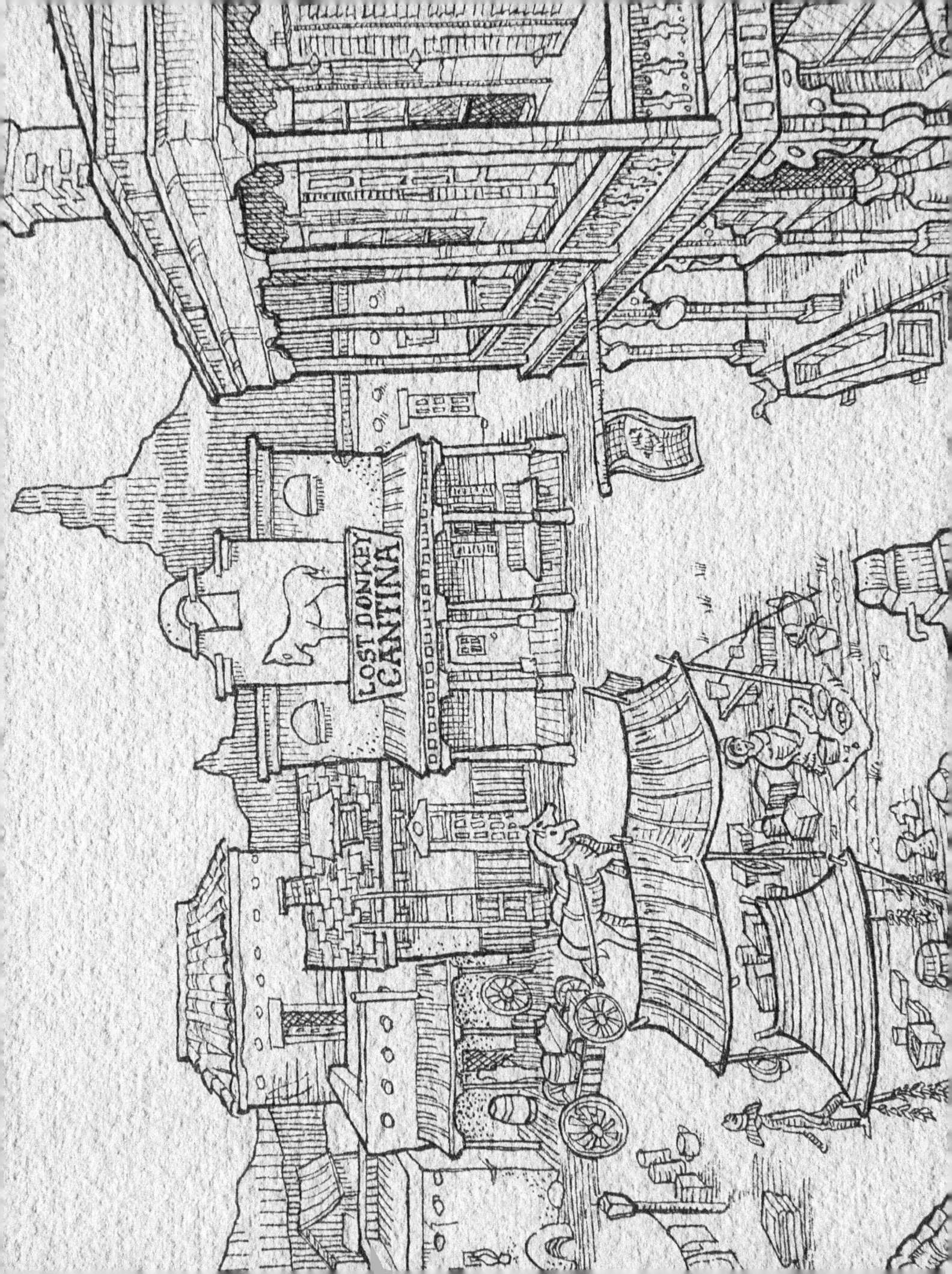

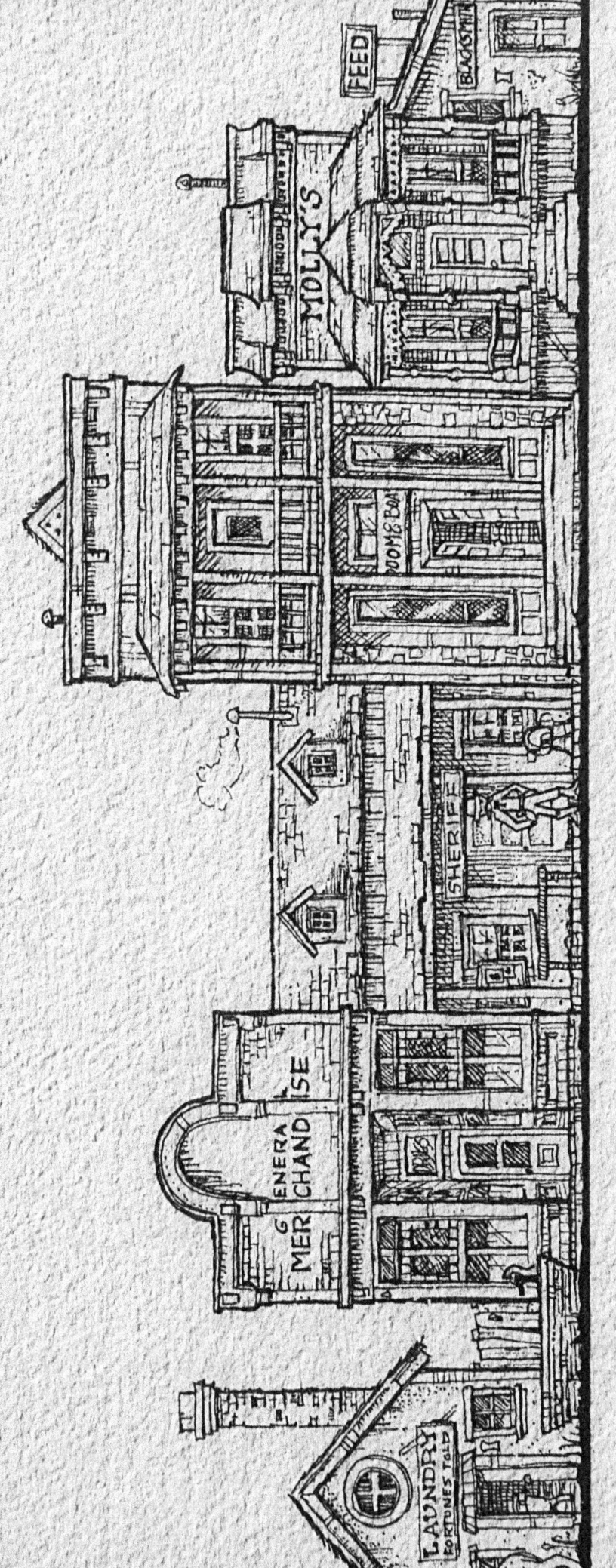

Front Street II, Wagon Wheel Gap, RedRock Canyon Territory

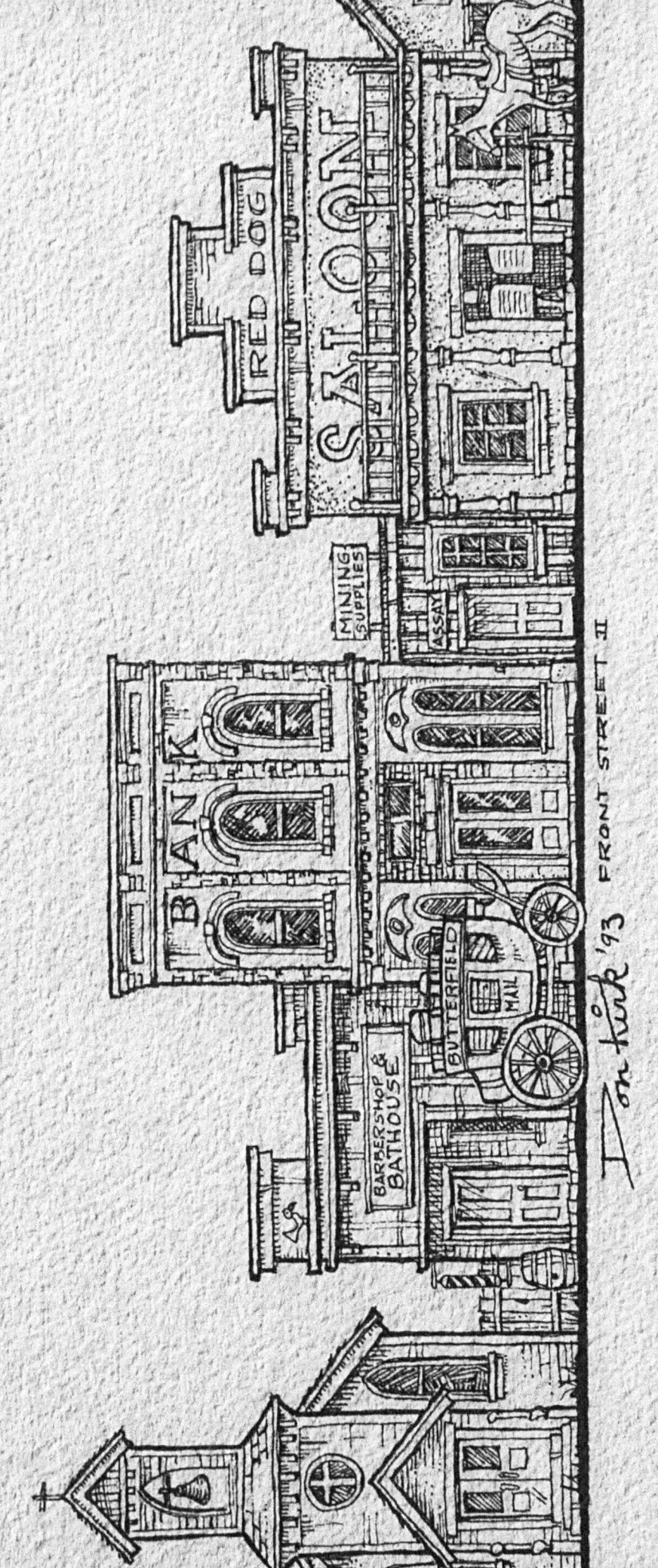

Front Street II, Wagon Wheel Gap, RedRock Canyon Territory

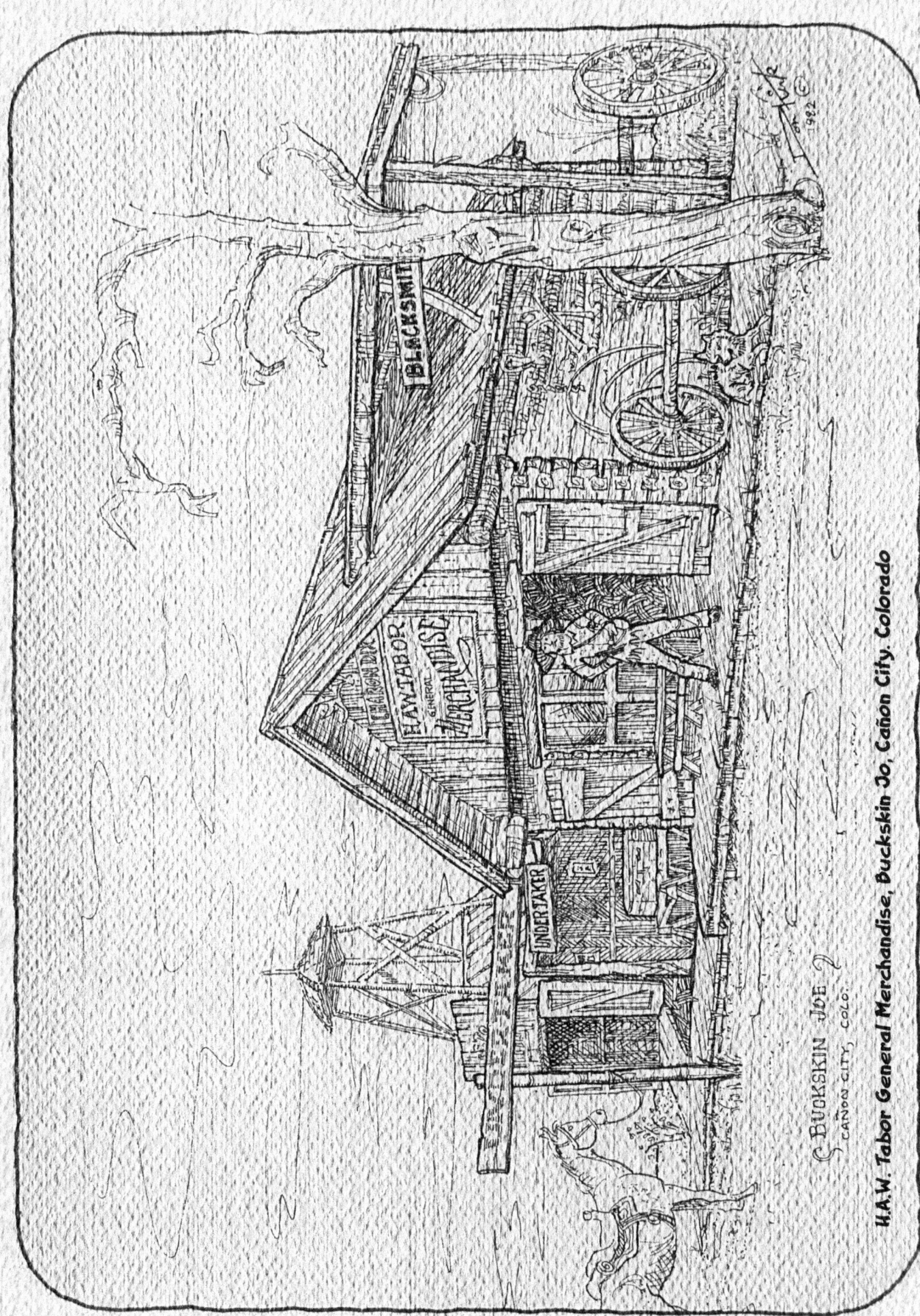

H.A.W. Tabor General Merchandise, Buckskin Jo, Cañon City, Colorado

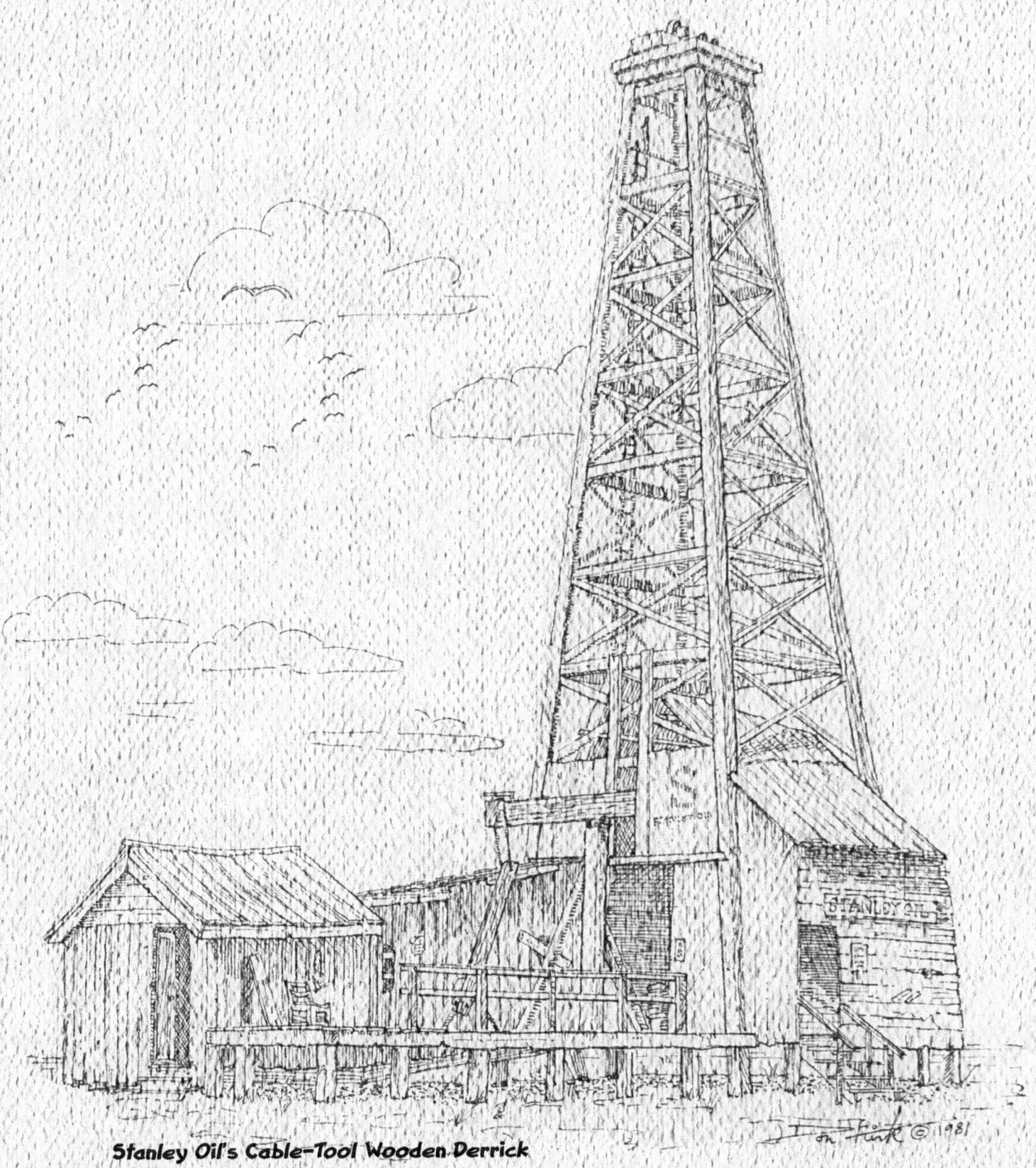

Stanley Oil's Cable-Tool Wooden Derrick

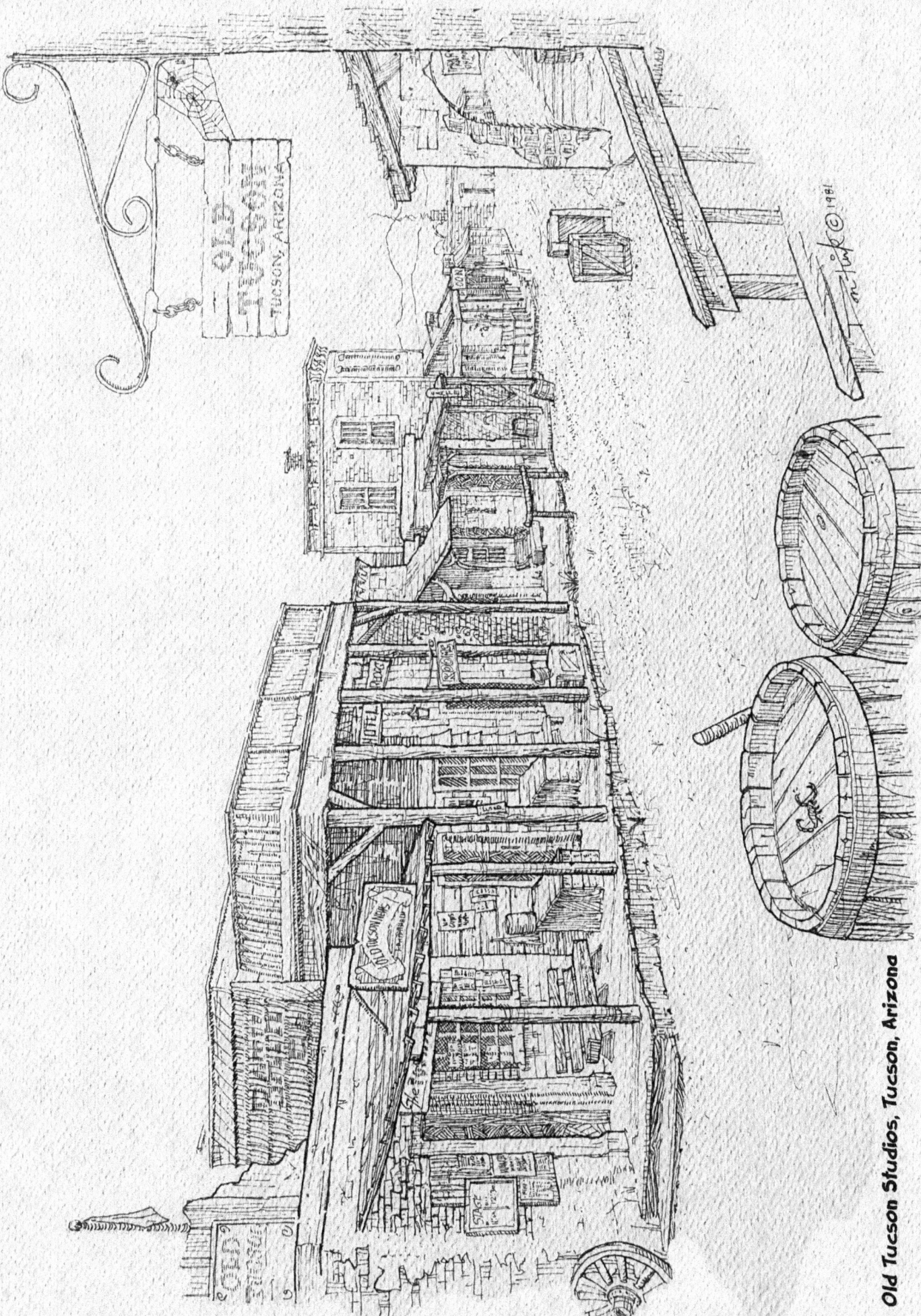

Old Tucson Studios, Tucson, Arizona

Snake Oil Salesman

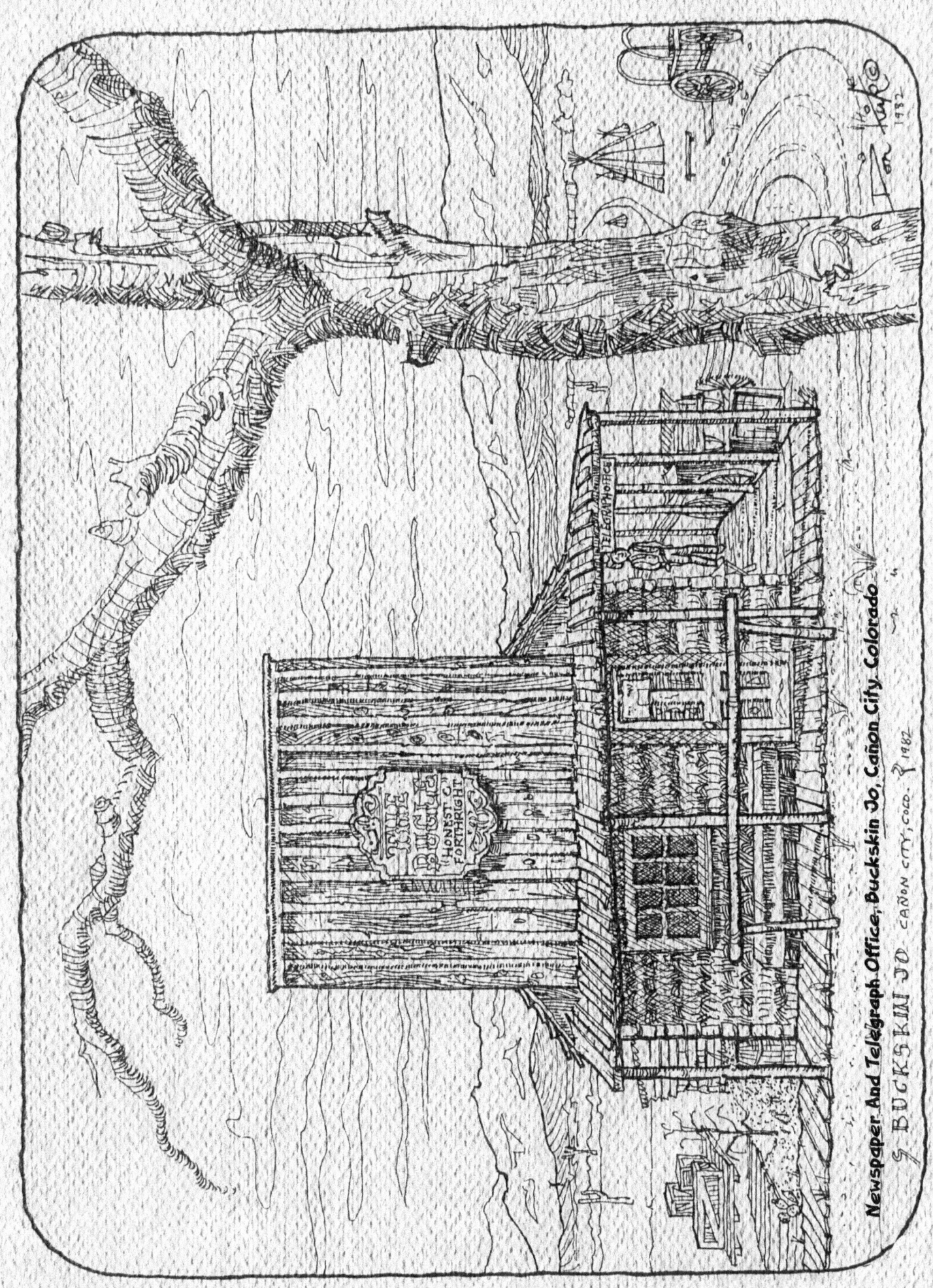

Newspaper And Telegraph Office, Buckskin Jo, Cañon City, Colorado

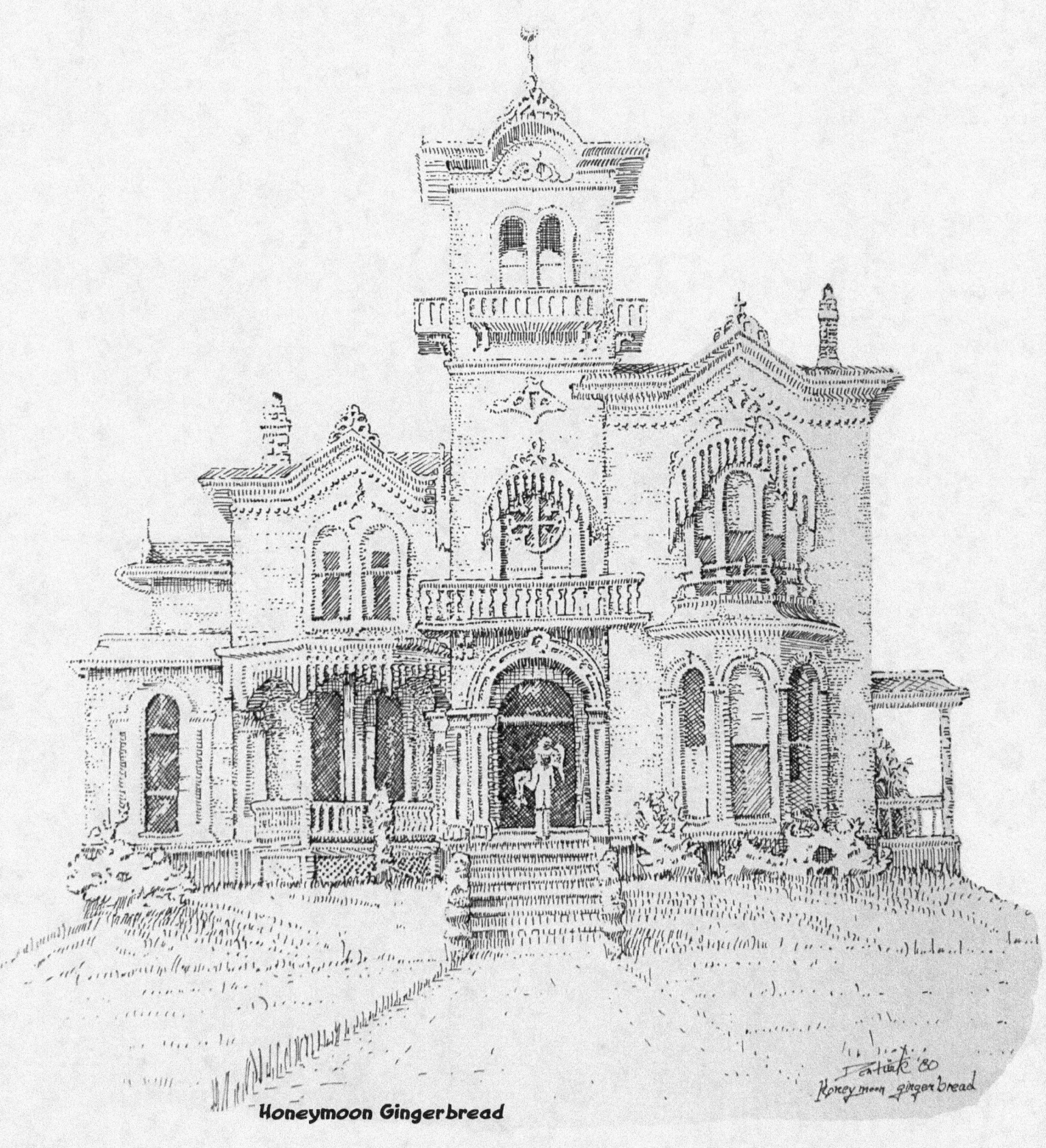

Honeymoon Gingerbread

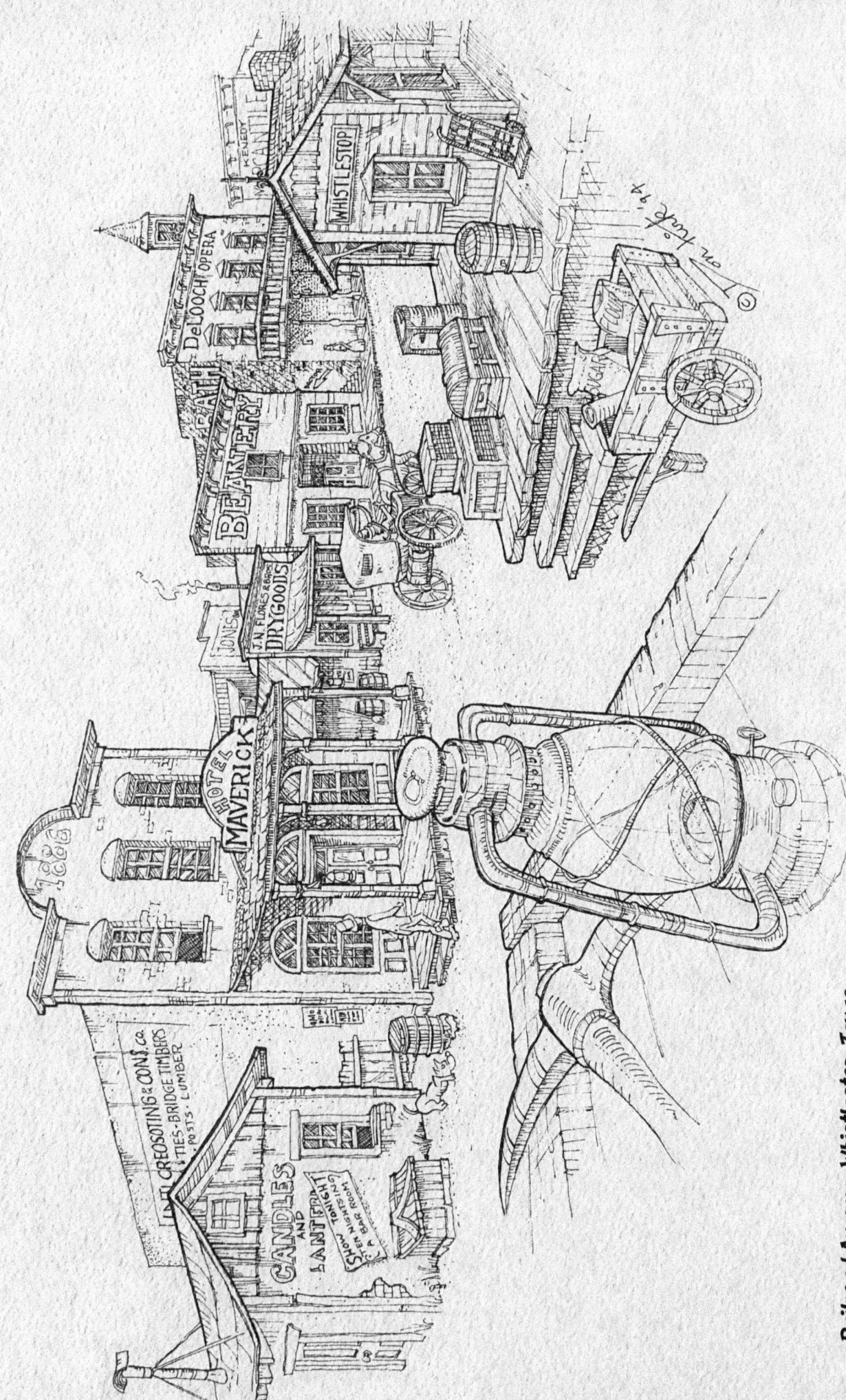

Railroad Avenue, Whistlestop, Texas

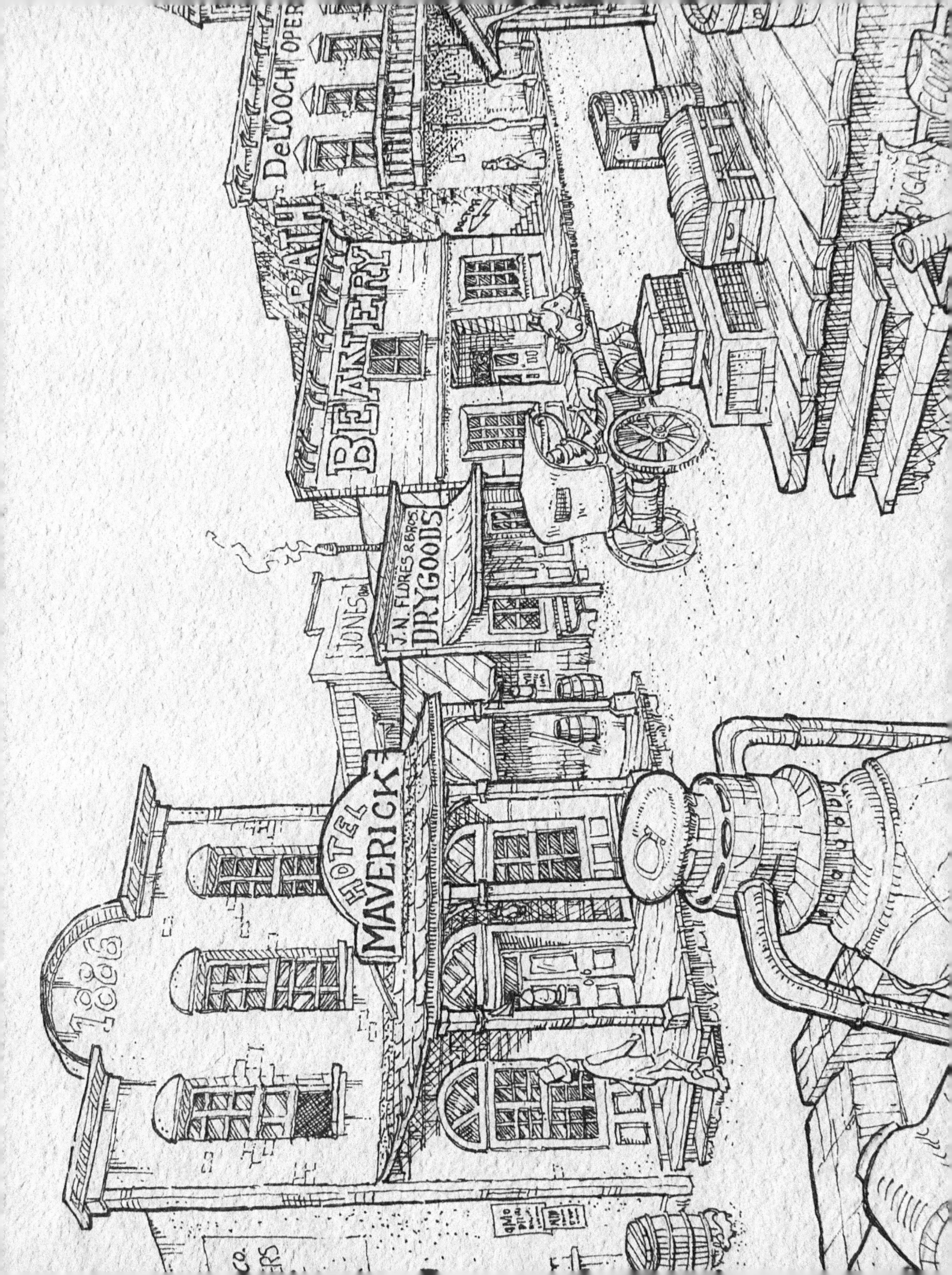

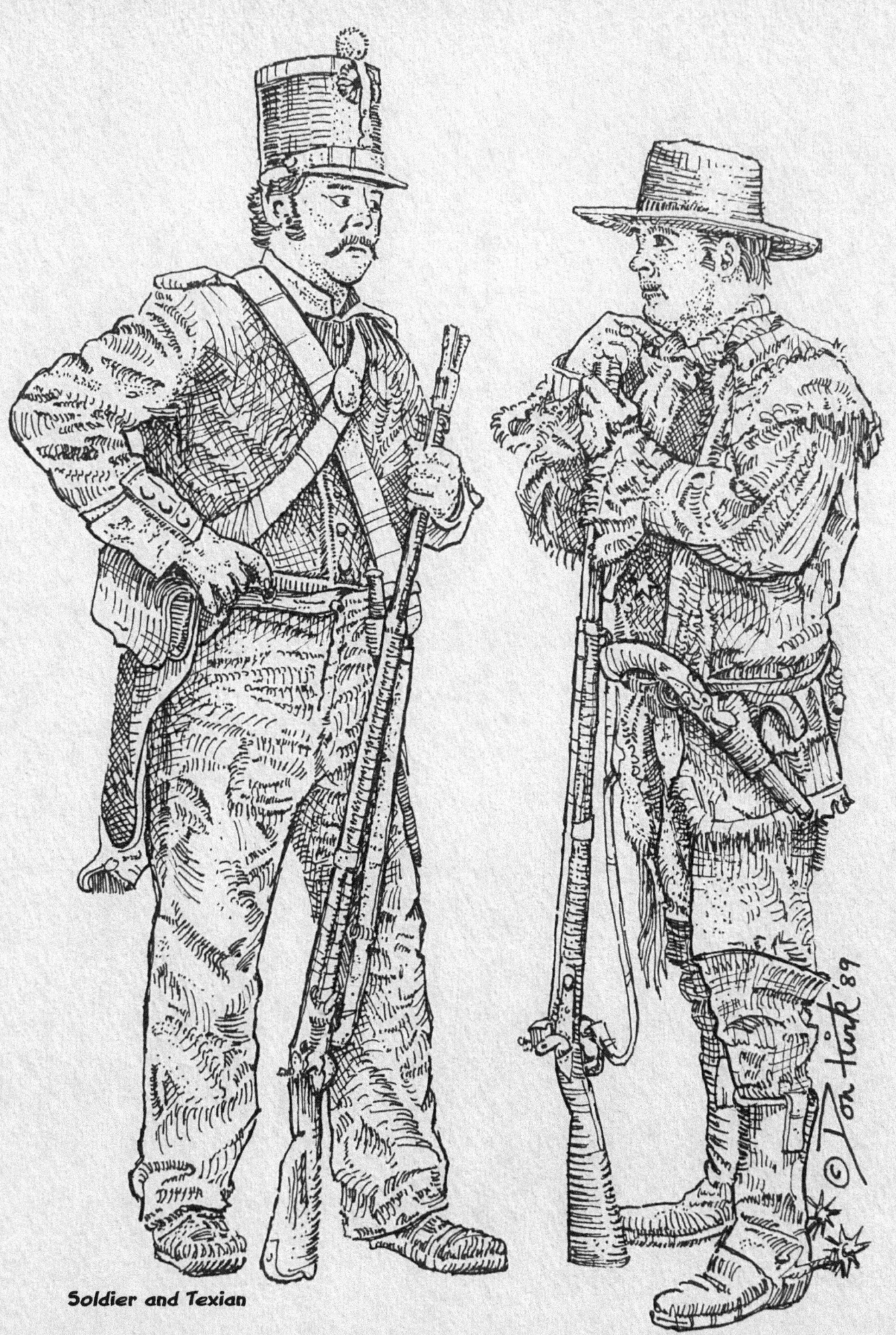

Soldier and Texian

Broken Spur Ranch, RedRock Canyon Territory

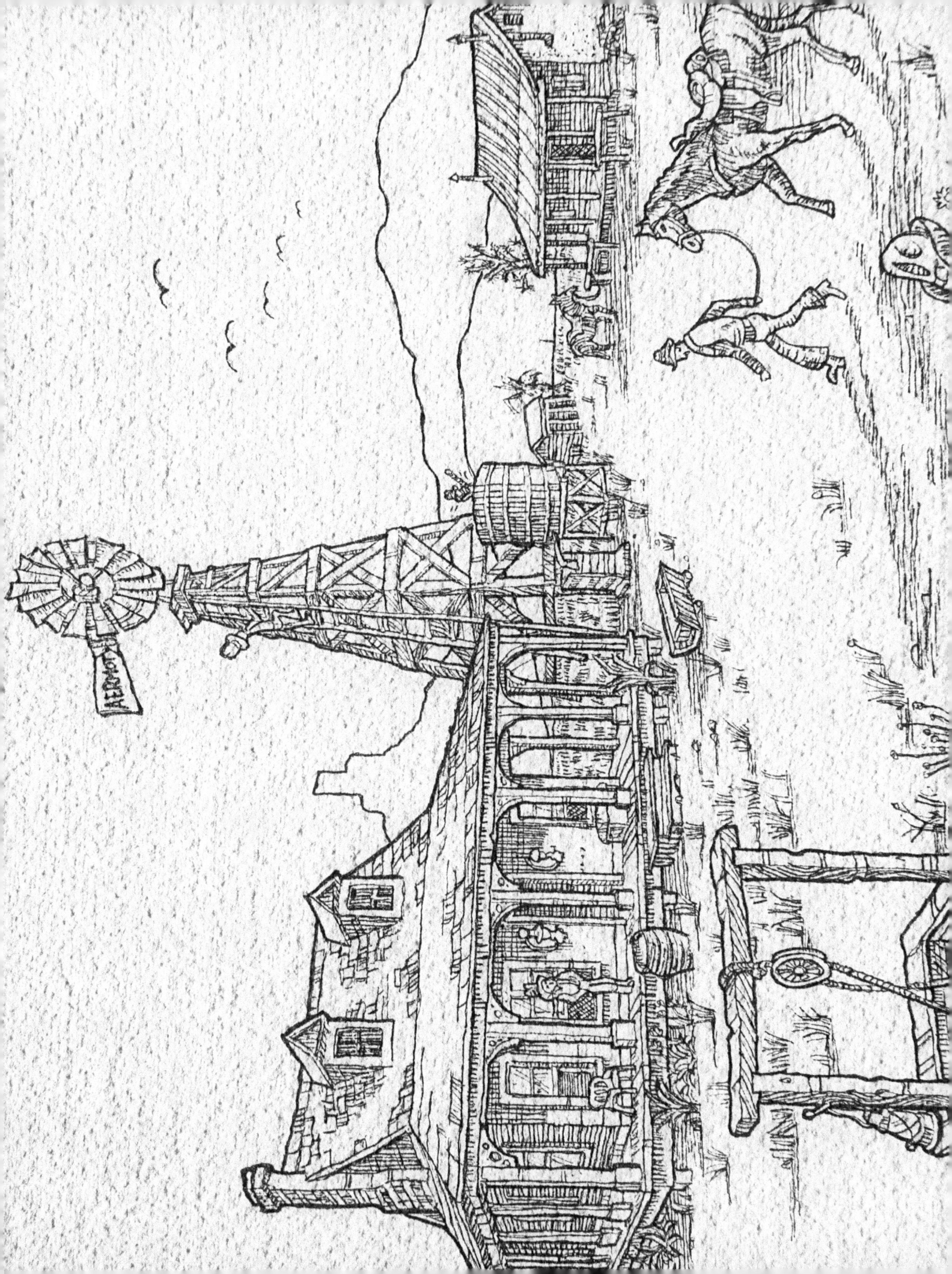

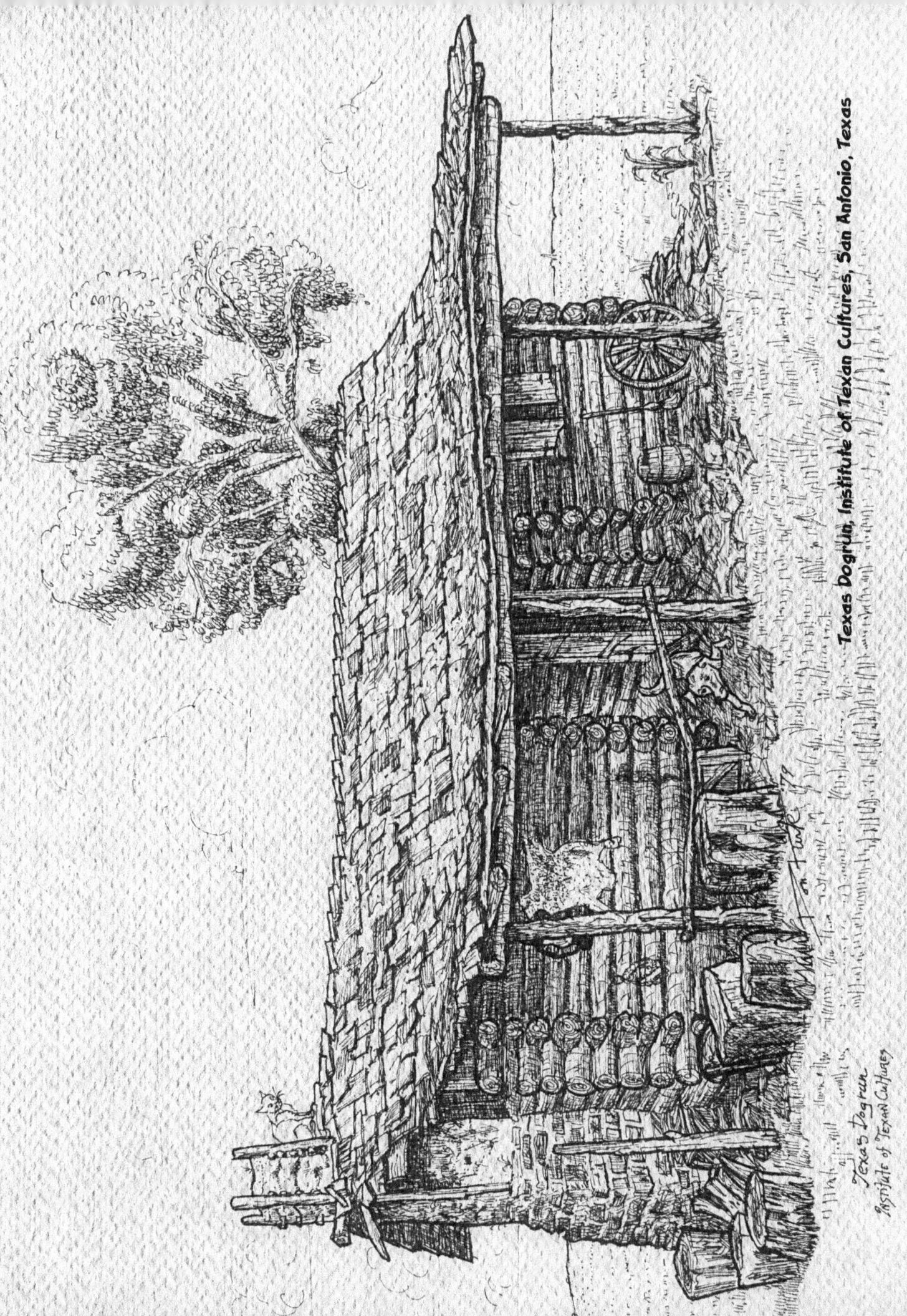

Texas Dogrun

Institute of Texan Cultures

Texas Dogrun, Institute of Texan Cultures, San Antonio, Texas

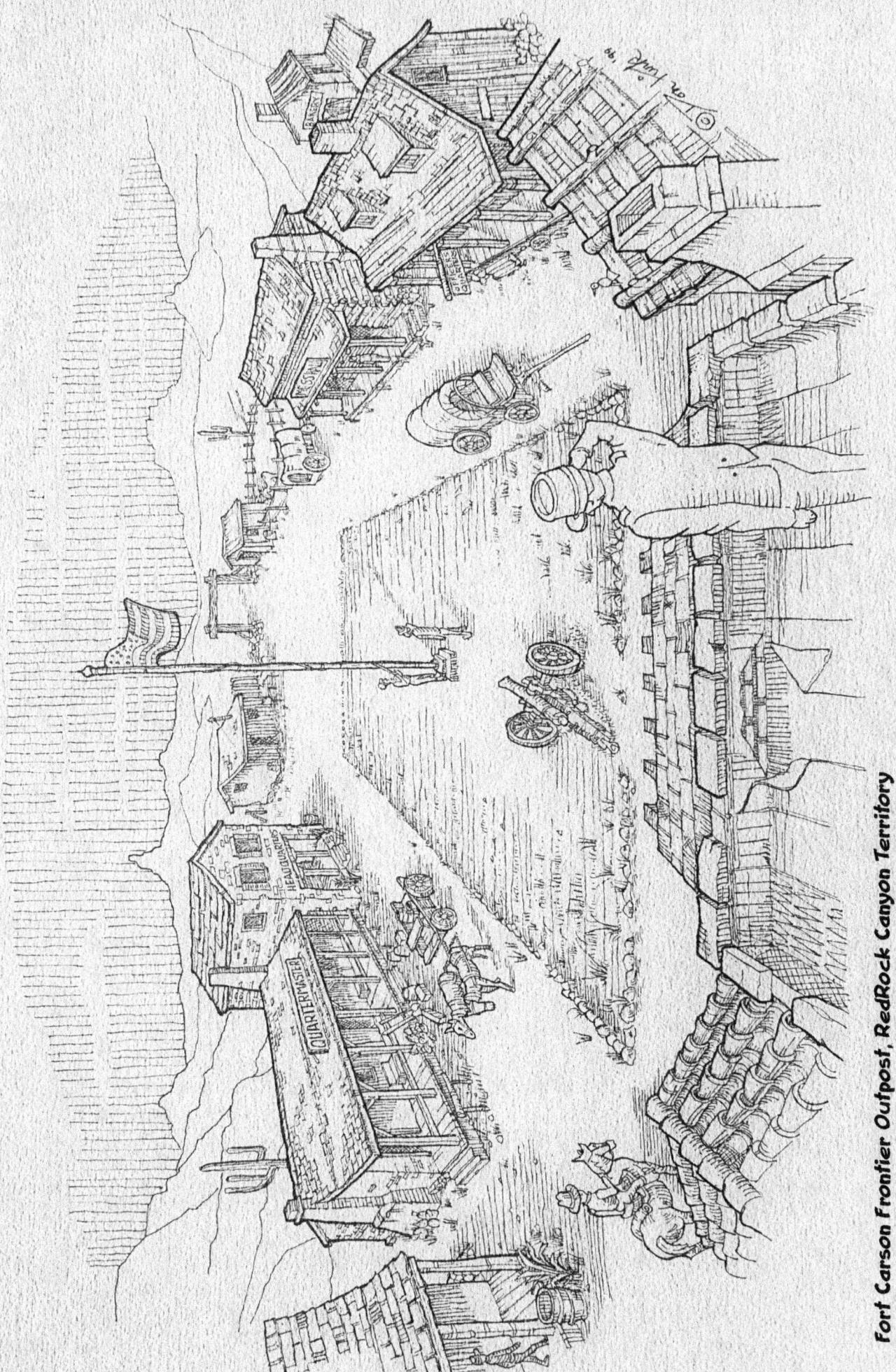

Fort Carson Frontier Outpost, RedRock Canyon Territory

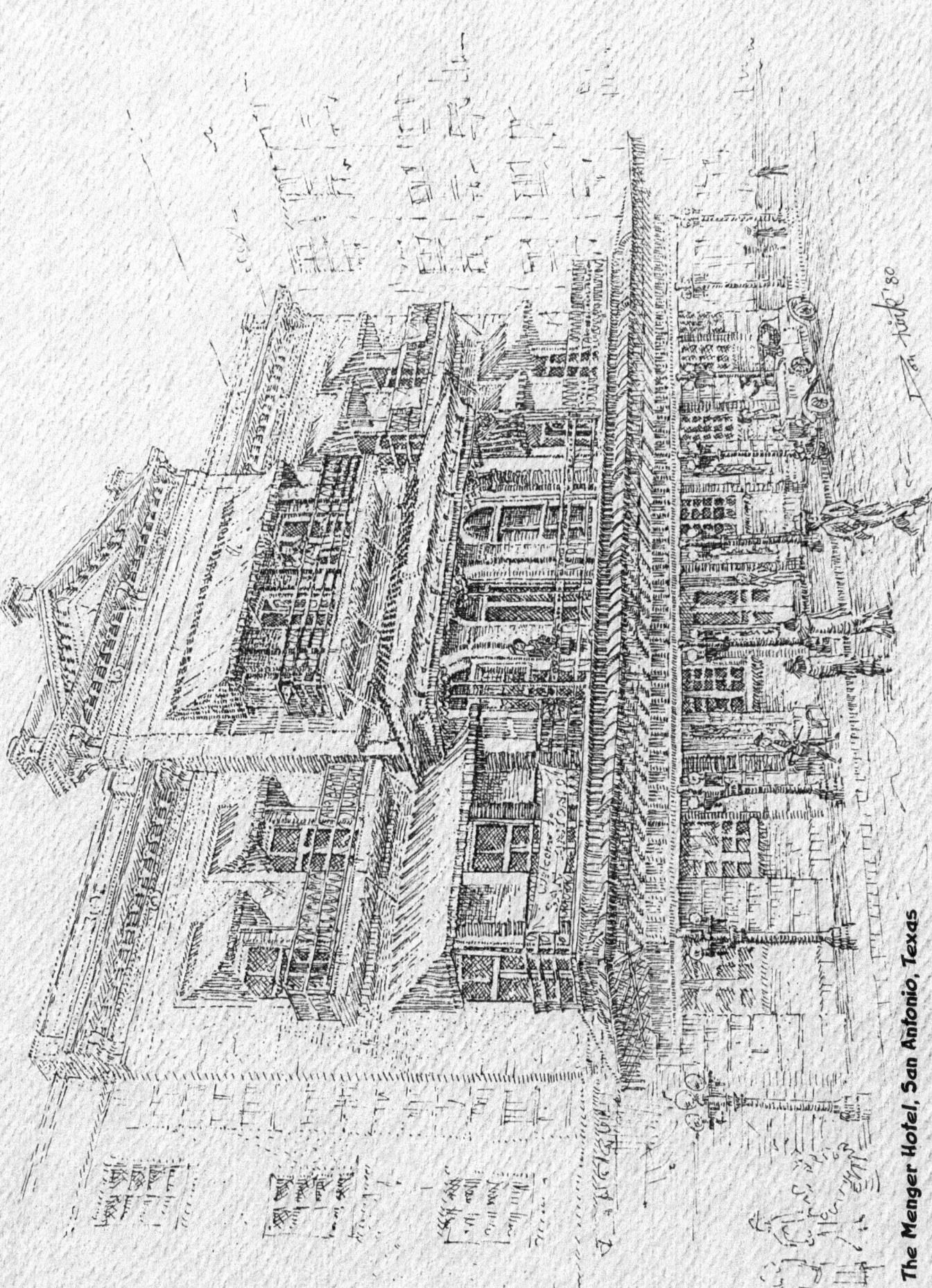

The Menger Hotel, San Antonio, Texas

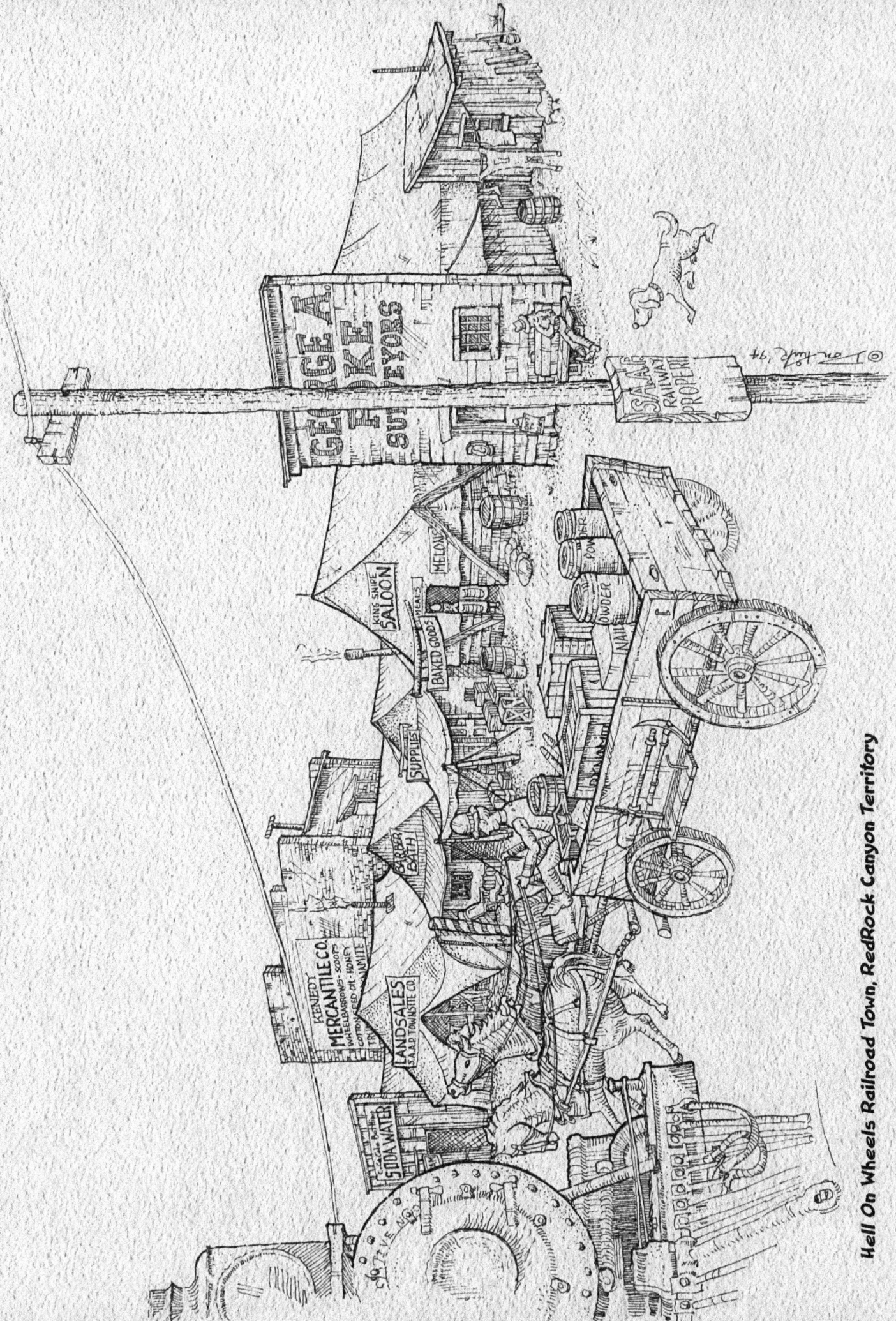

Hell On Wheels Railroad Town, RedRock Canyon Territory

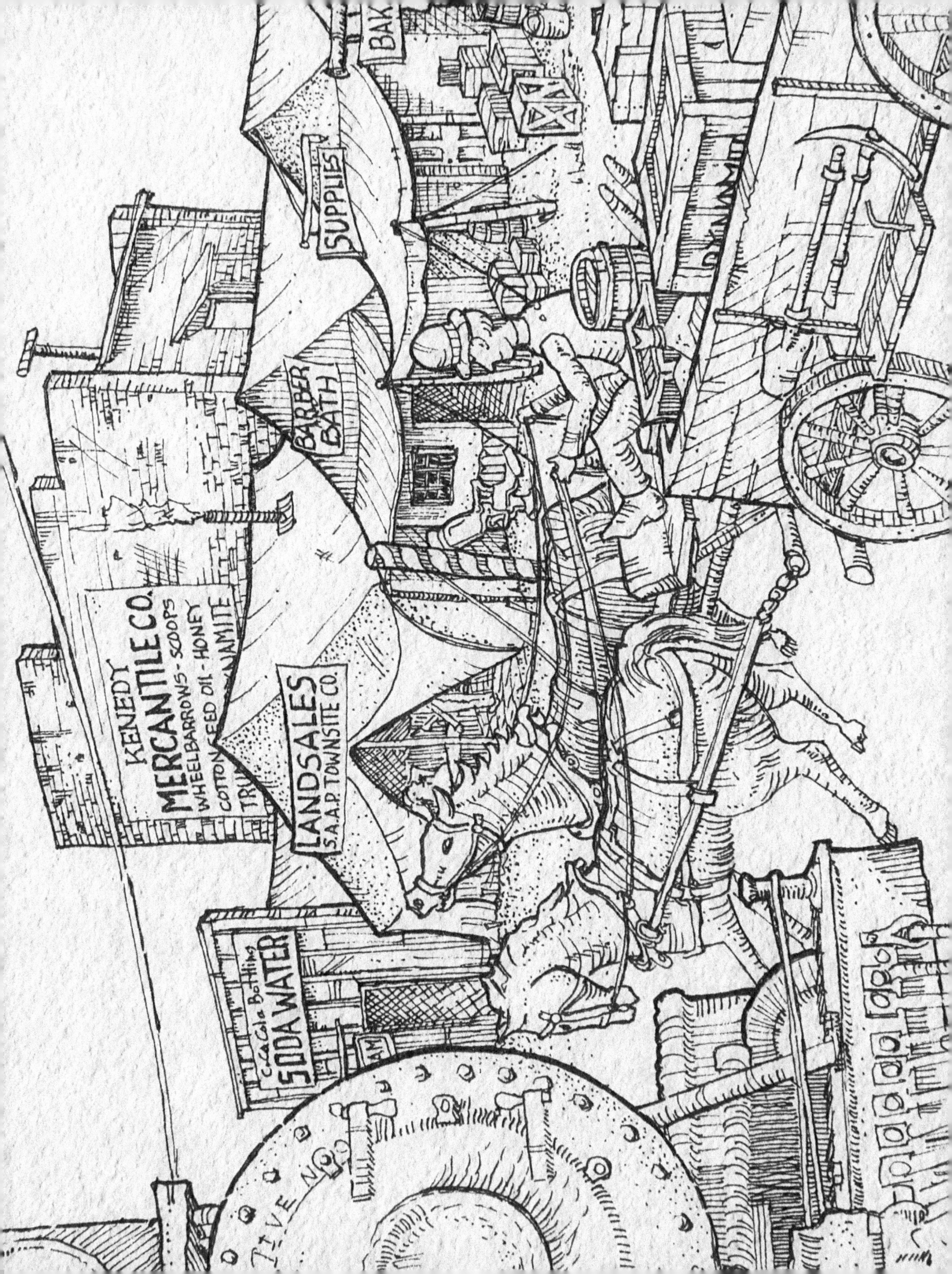

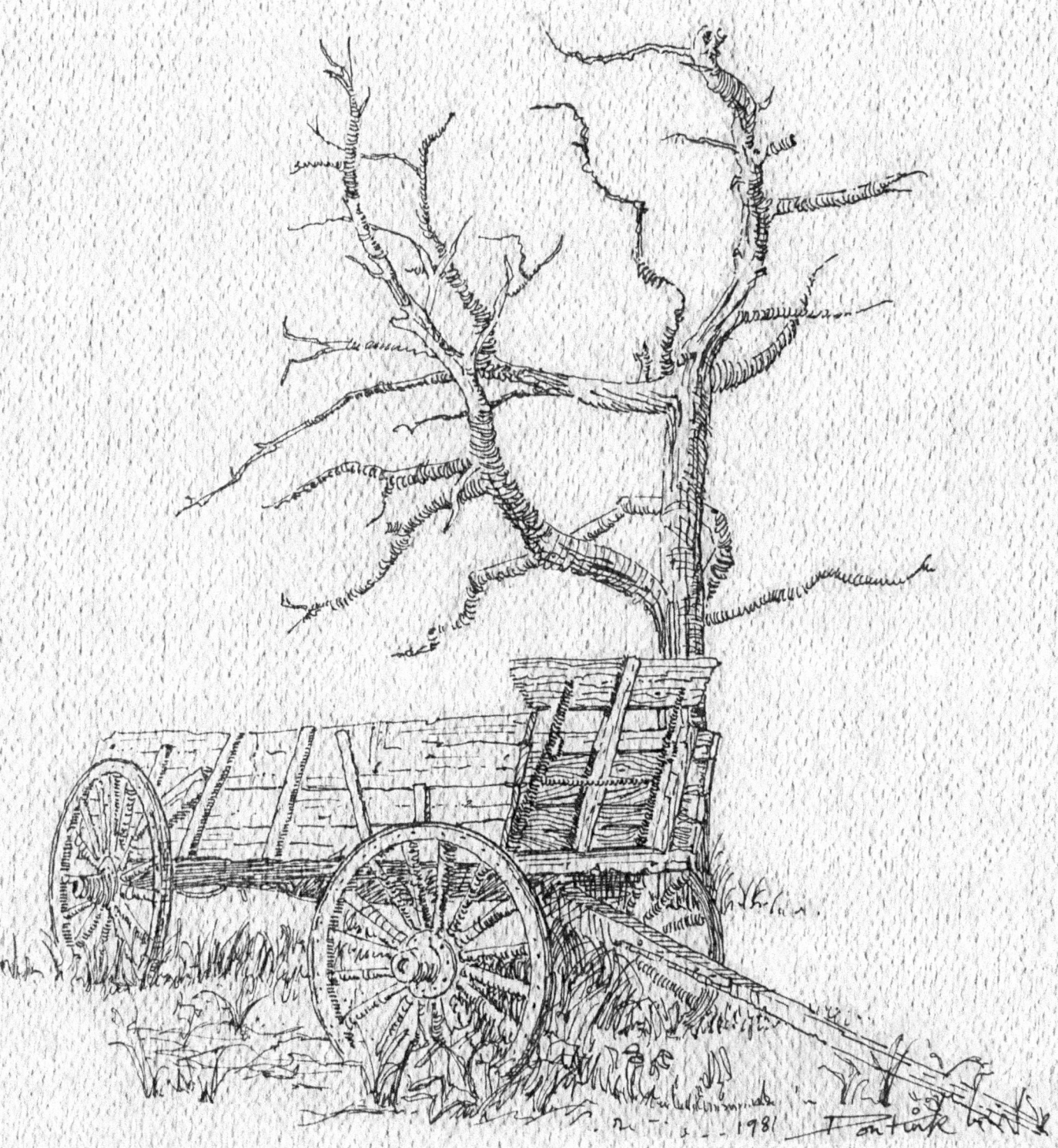

1981

A Lonely Nowhere

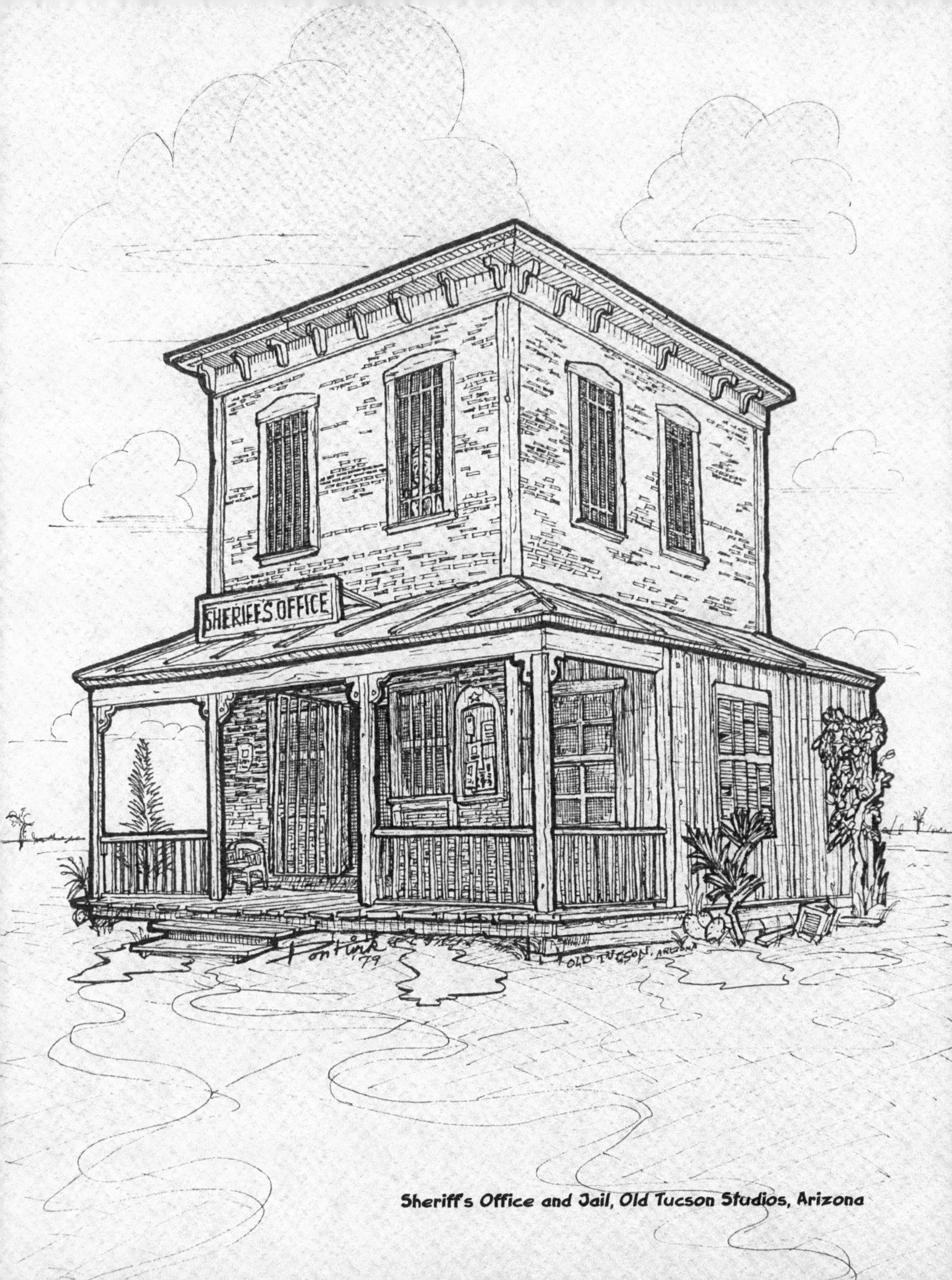

SHERIFF'S OFFICE

Sheriff's Office and Jail, Old Tucson Studios, Arizona

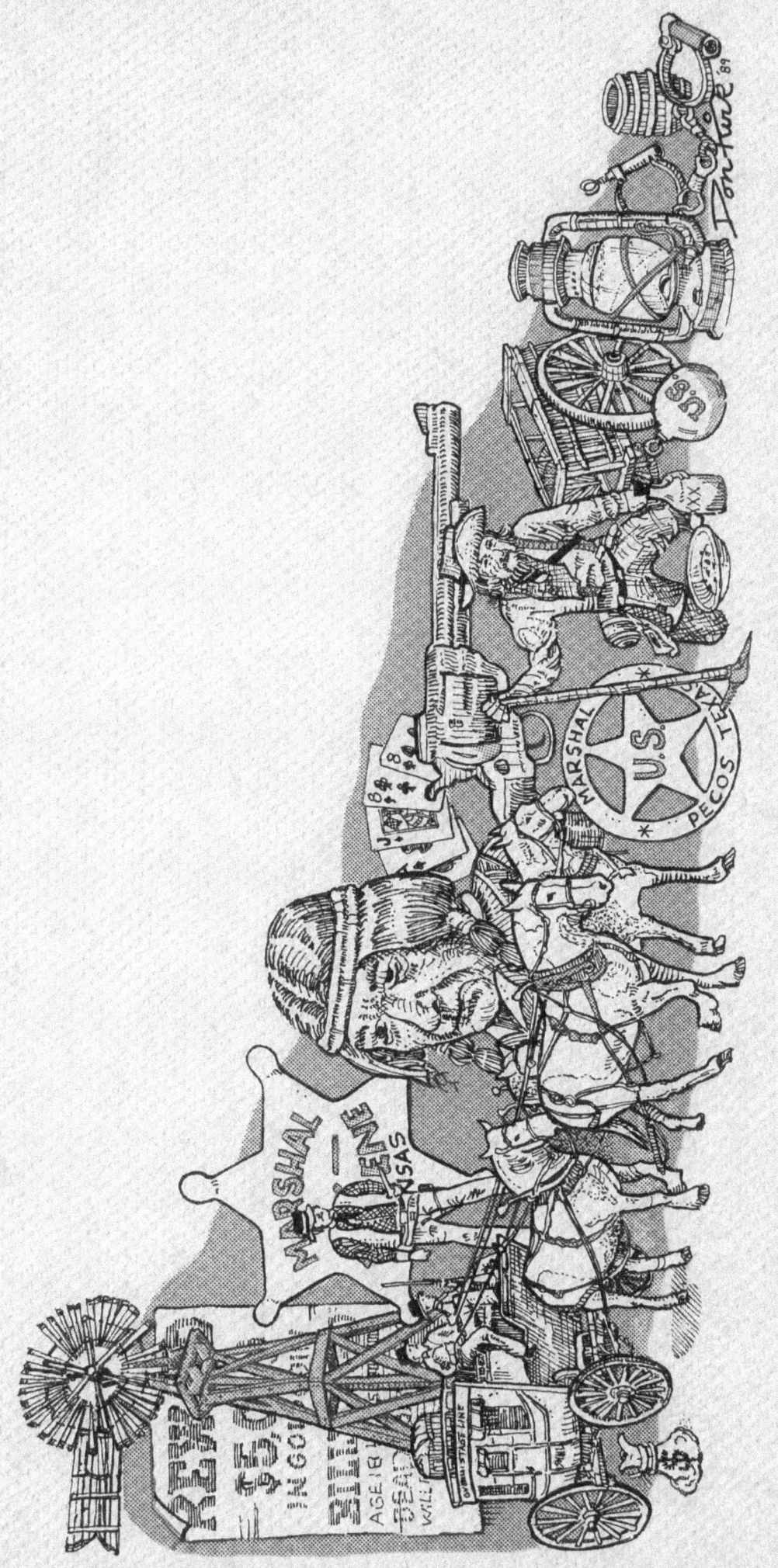

Symbols Of The American West

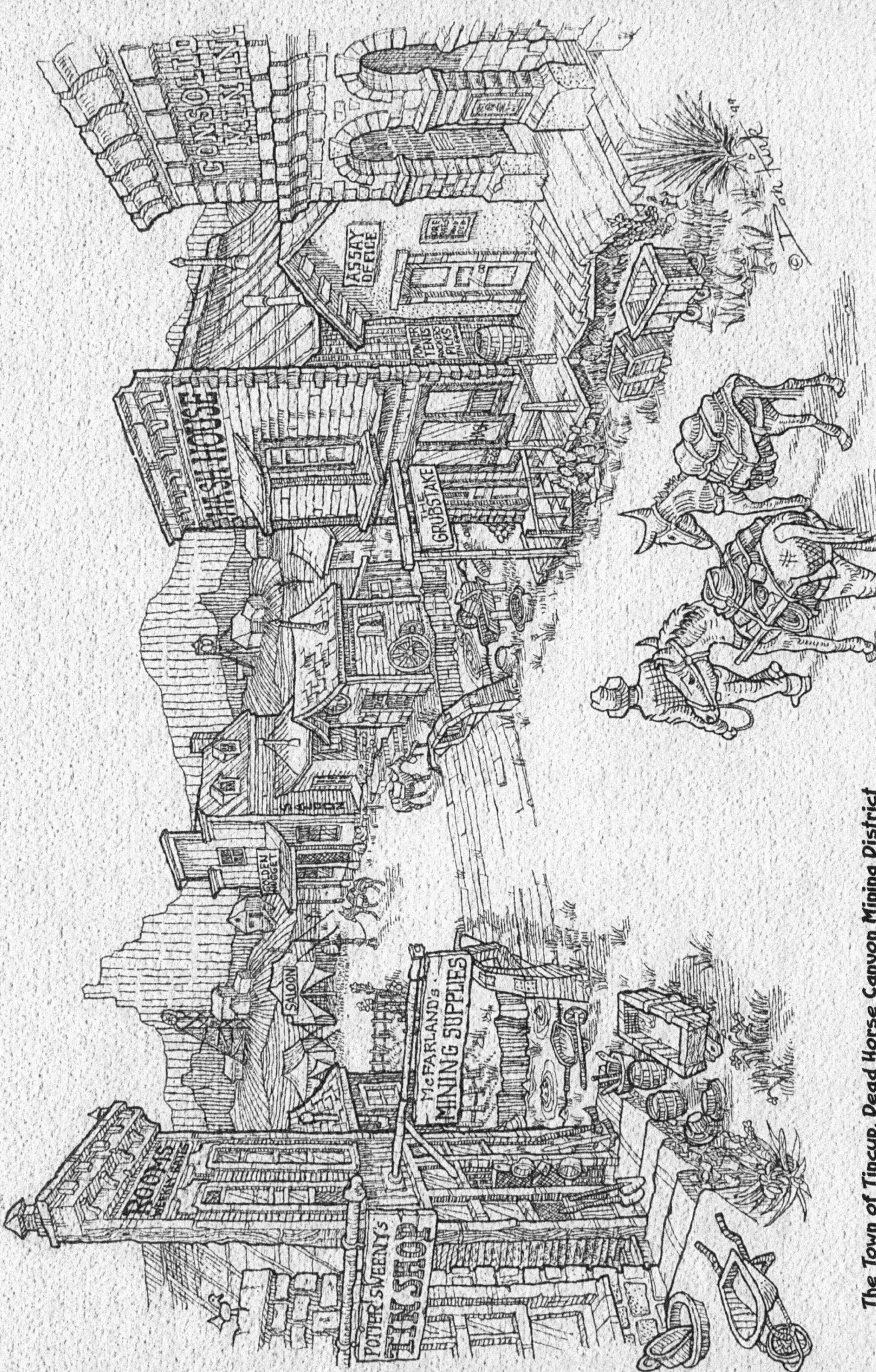

The Town of Tincup, Dead Horse Canyon Mining District

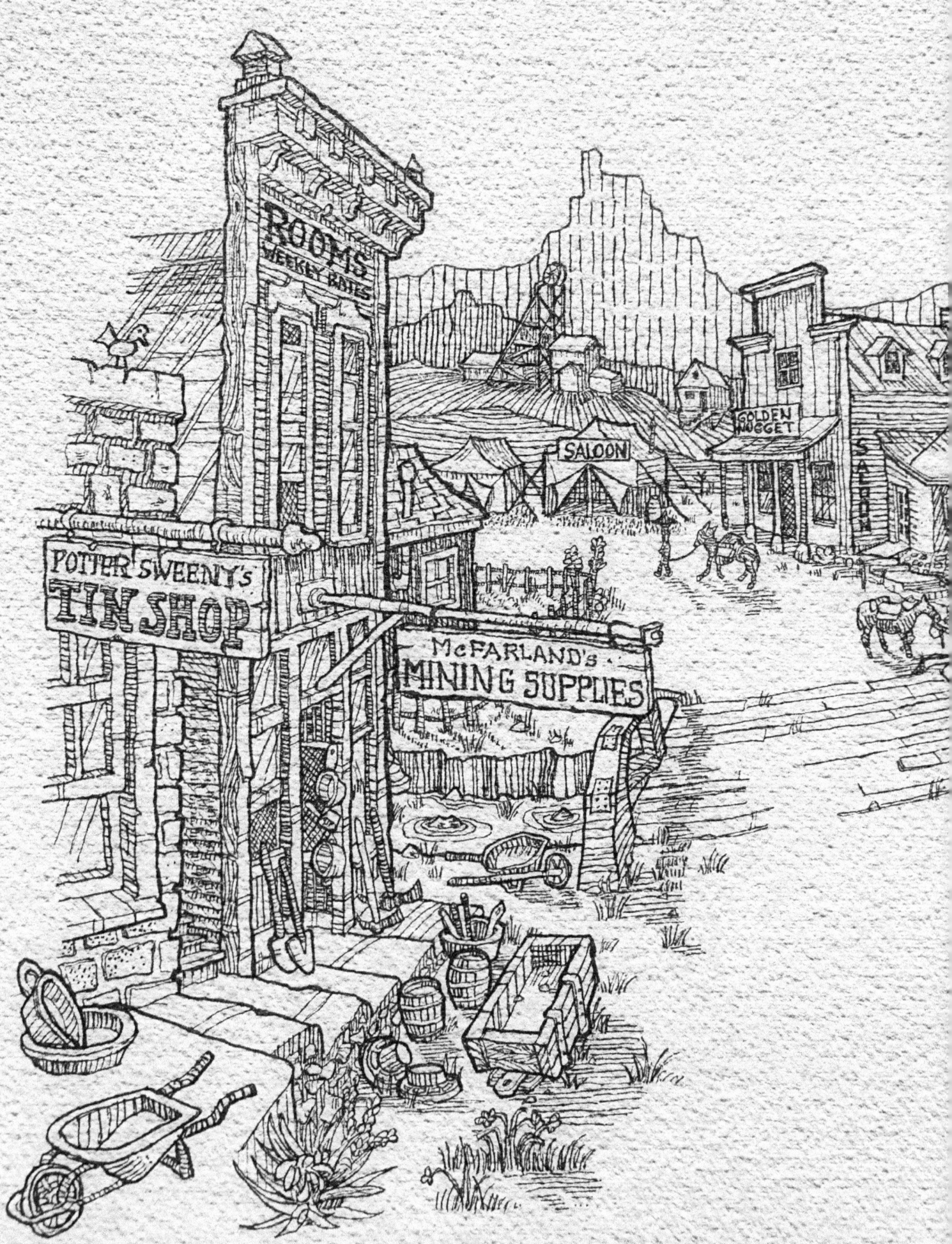

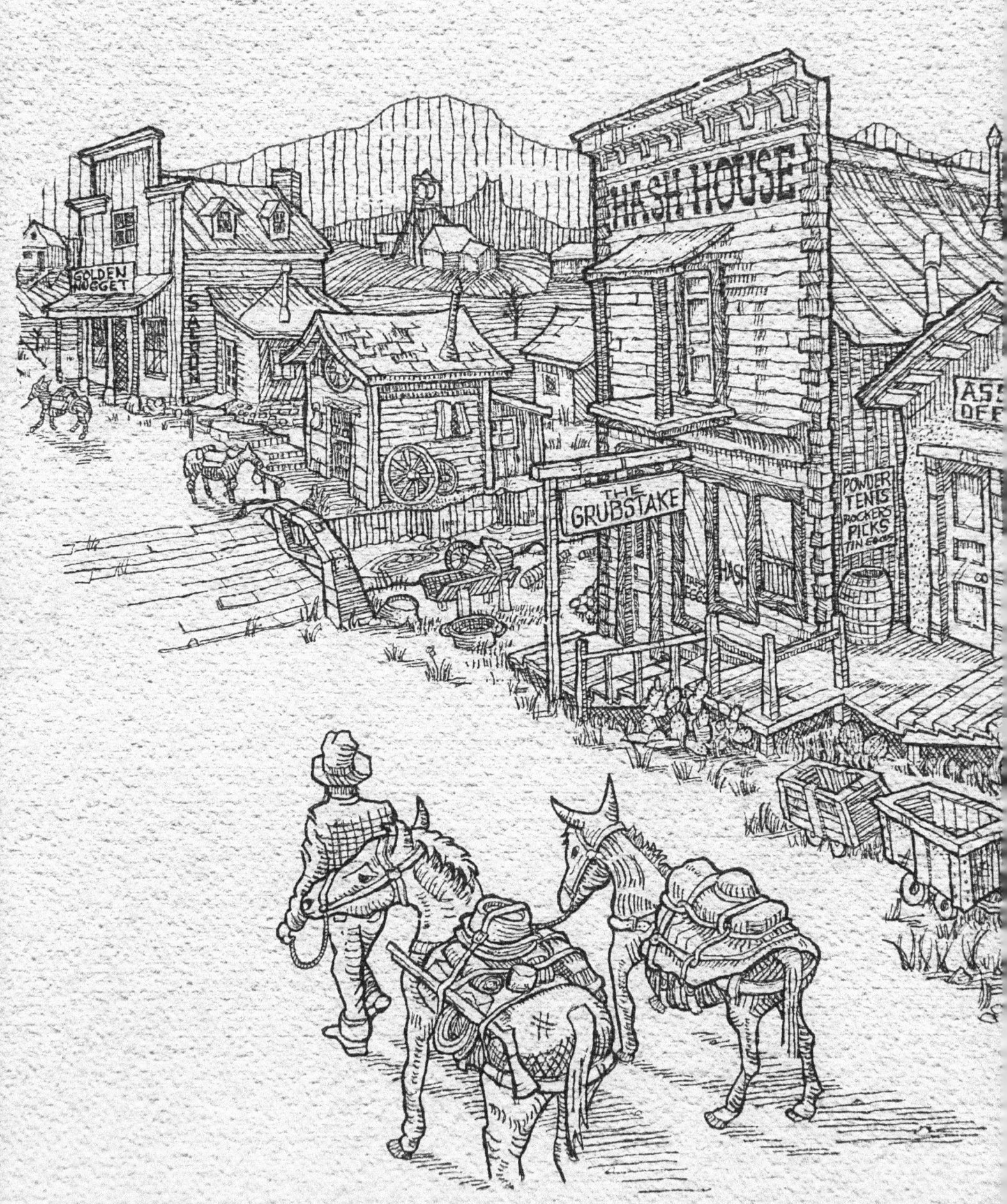

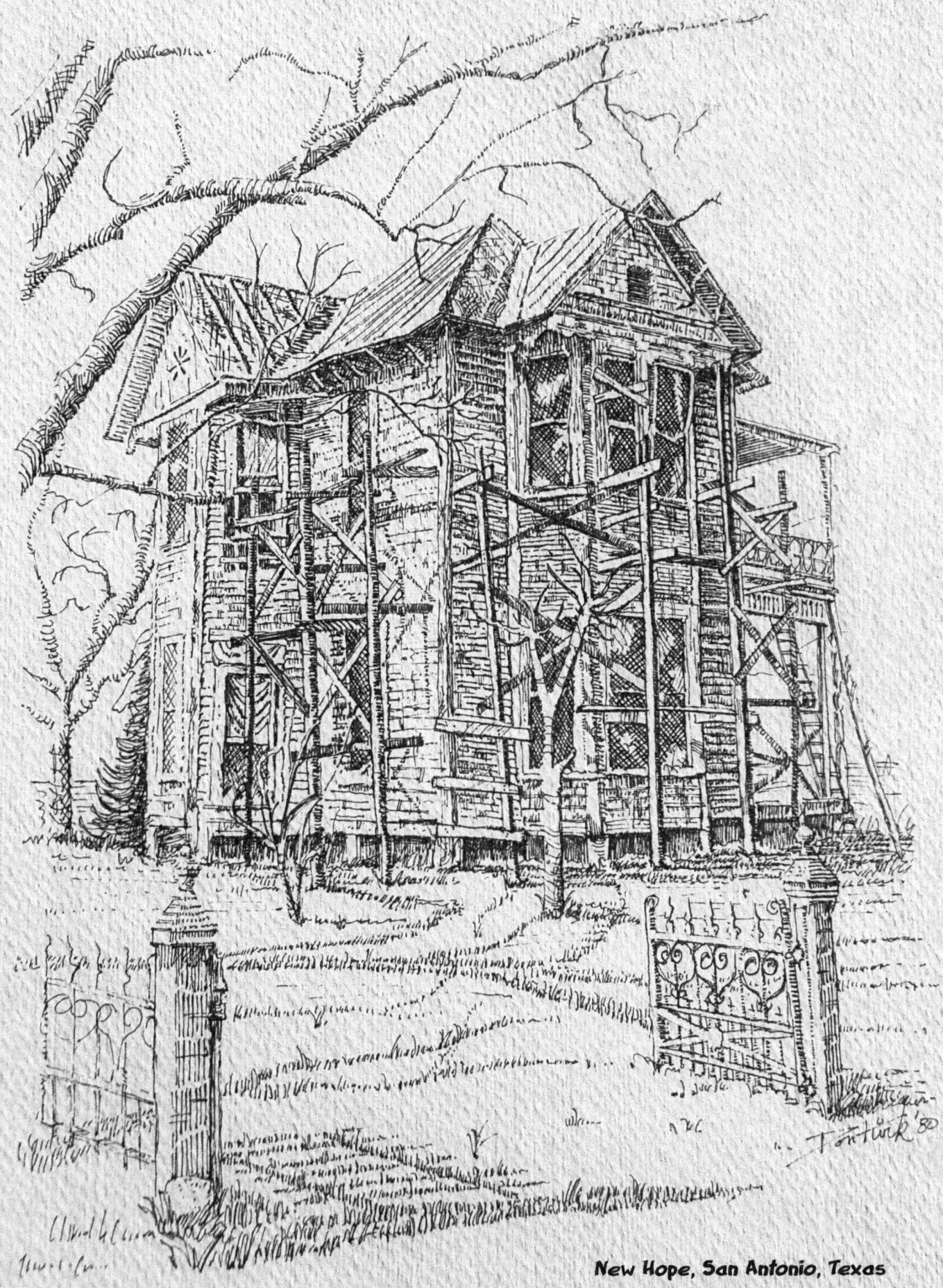

New Hope, San Antonio, Texas

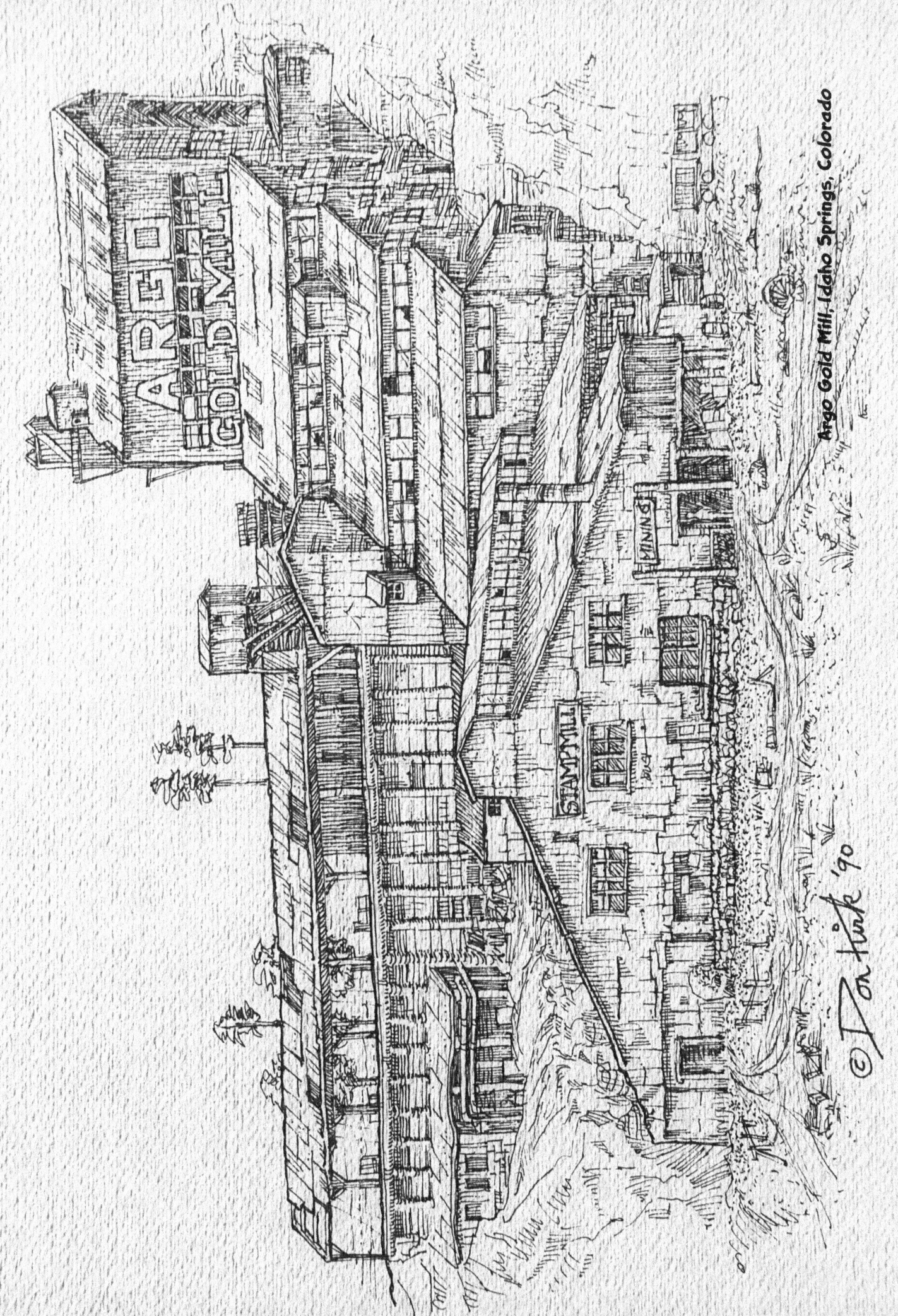

Argo Gold Mill, Idaho Springs, Colorado

© Don Kurtz '90

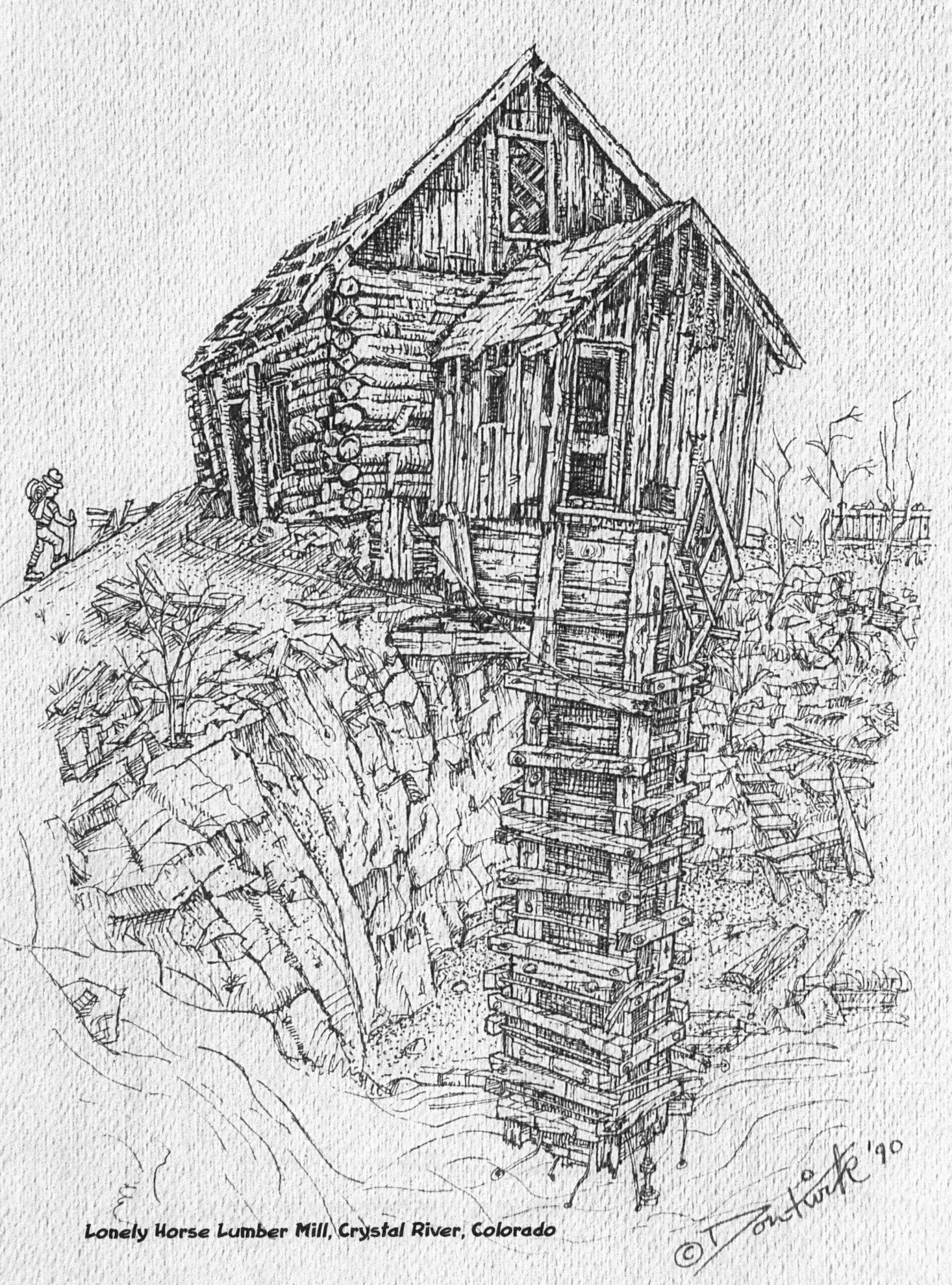

Lonely Horse Lumber Mill, Crystal River, Colorado

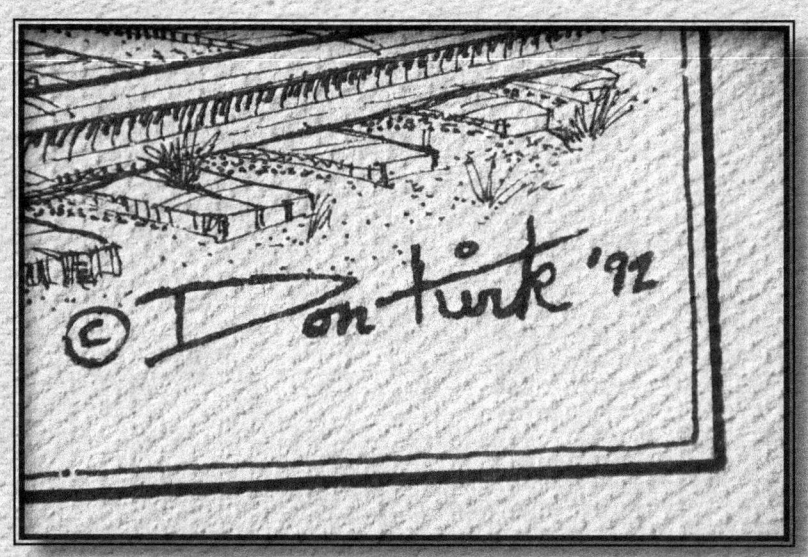

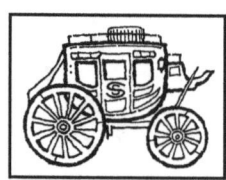

ISBN 978-0-9898004-5-7

www.ingramcontent.com/pod-product-compliance
Lightning Source LLC
Chambersburg PA
CBHW080952170526
45158CB00008B/2450